GW00862437

LADY

essential
P A R T Y G U I D E

The definitive guide to London dining & events

How to use this guide...

In this guide you will find the very best of London's dining, going out, entertainment and hospitality scene, together with the best companies for hosting parties and events.

Curated by **Lady Blonde** – the leading lady when it comes to knowing what's what on the London scene – **Lady Blonde's Essential Party Guide** is the go-to handbook for discerning Londoners seeking dining and event solutions.

On pages 10 – 25, **Lady Blonde** recommends her favourite venues and services for specific occasions and requirements. Pages 26 – 122 hold further details on all the venues and companies referenced and you can also search for venues via the chart on pages 124 – 127.

So if you've ever wanted to know where to go on a date, where to impress a client or endure the in-laws, where to celebrate a birthday or host a corporate event with a difference, this guide has all the solutions you need. And it doesn't end there: you can find more information on **LadyBlonde.com**.

CLS MEDIA LIMITED
020 7221 0983 · LBHQ@ladyblonde.com · www.ladyblonde.com

Publisher: CLS Media Ltd · **Editor:** Claudia Shapiro · **Chief Contributor:** Lady Blonde
Head of Design: Erin Lock Lee · **Head of Sales:** Gwenyth Hardiman
Editorial Coordinator: Harriet Dobree

PARTNERS

EDITOR'S NOTE

With more Michelin-starred restaurants in London than there are weeks in the year (and countless other bars, restaurants, venues and opportunities to explore), discerning Londoners are simultaneously blessed and overwhelmed with choice. This guide, together with **LadyBlonde.com**, has been designed to make things simple. If you like the finer (and sexier) things in life, this guide makes all the decisions for you.

Claudia

Claudia Shapiro, Editor

CONTENTS

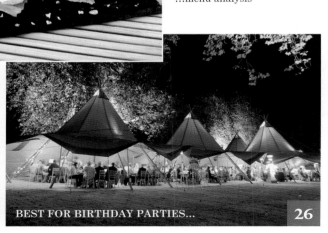

22

BEST FOR BIRTHDAY PARTIES...   **26**

CONCIERGE

London under review...

Lady Blonde sends weekly e-newsletters, including a lead review and latest news, keeping subscribers up-to-date on the London scene.

Known for her witty, sharp and unpretentious reflections on the places she has visited, Lady Blonde offers absorbing and valuable insight into London's finest destinations (and a peek into her sometimes glamorous, sometimes ludicrous daily life). The reviews always manage to inspire and excite, encapsulating what a particular place is good for, be that dinner with a date, lunch with the in-laws or a coffee with your bank manager. And no time is wasted on places that are not up to standard – with so many wonderful places to visit, why waste time reading about the ones you shouldn't?

And finally, the e-newsletters offer bite-size information (see right) to keep the savviest Londoners up-to-date and in-the-know.

Subscribe today: LadyBlonde.com

NEW OPENINGS

Be the first to hear about London's newest hotspots.

FAVOURITES

Be inspired by Lady Blonde's favourite places.

DEALS

Receive exclusive subscriber offers and deals.

EVENTS

Find out about upcoming parties and events.

COMPETITIONS

Enter competitions to win fabulous prizes worth over £200.

Subscribe today. LadyBlonde.com

SUBSCRIBE to Lady Blonde's weekly newsletter at LadyBlonde.com

Calling all social(media)ites...

Keep up with the life and whereabouts of Lady Blonde by following her on Twitter and Facebook.

facebook.com/theLadyBlonde
twitter.com/theLadyBlonde

Be inspired. Stay informed.
Delivered to your inbox every Friday

A peek into London's finest...

LadyBlonde.com – designed to connect the savviest of Londoners with the very best London has to offer – now operates an exclusive membership facility for carefully selected, discerning individuals.

There are two tiers of membership: **LB2C** is for aspirational Londoners who want to stay in the know; **LB2B** is a dedicated Concierge Service designed for those who go out and entertain frequently for both business and pleasure. For **LB2B Members**, membership of **LadyBlonde.com** is like having the most reliable, well-connected and resourceful PA (or PA for their PAs) with one hell of an address book and unrivalled expertise. From last minute priority table-bookings, to bespoke hospitality packages and event planning, Lady Blonde's team has it covered. See over for more details.

Register interest today at LadyBlonde.com/members

MEMBERSHIP

Membership of **LadyBlonde.com** is by-invitation-only but you can register your interest to receive an application form.

To register interest for membership of Lady Blonde.com and the Concierge Service, scan the QR code below or visit:

LadyBlonde.com/ members

SCANNING QR CODES

Scan the code below to visit LadyBlonde.com NOW

WHAT? A QR is a 2D bar code that can be read by your smart phone. It contains a URL weblink which you will be directed to within seconds, when you scan it with your smartphone. So there's no need to type in any info; just scan the code and away you go.

HOW? If you don't already have a QR reader on your smart phone, you can download one cost-free and quickly from any App Store. Once this is done, with the reader open on your phone, point the camera at the code. Hold your hand steady, and the reader will automatically snap the picture for you, and direct you straight to the link.

WHO FOR? QR Readers are available in all App Stores and are compatible with the iPhone, Blackberry and Android devices.

I'm a member of
LADY BLONDE'S CONCIERGE SERVICE
and I need help arranging...

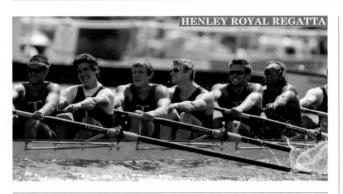

HENLEY ROYAL REGATTA

HOSPITALITY FOR THE SOCIAL SEASON

*Attending one of the UK's leading social occasions
combines sport, Champagne and glamour for a fun
day out to remember. From stand-alone tickets and
hospitality packages, to VIP passes and picnics,
Lady Blonde can arrange it all for LB2B Members.*

Polo in the Park
3RD – 5TH JUNE

Royal Ascot
14TH – 18TH JUNE

Henley Royal Regatta
29TH JUNE – 3RD JULY

Veuve Clicquot Gold Cup
17TH JULY

Cartier Polo
24TH JULY

Glorious Goodwood
26TH – 30TH JULY

Cowes Week
6TH – 13TH AUGUST

Goodwood Revival
16TH – 18TH SEPTEMBER

Frieze Art Fair
13TH – 16TH OCTOBER

CARTIER POLO

A BESPOKE VIP FESTIVAL PACKAGE

*Love the music and the
atmosphere but not
so keen on camping?
Lady Blonde knows
a solution.*

Glyndebourne
21ST MAY – 28TH AUGUST

Isle of Wight Festival
10TH – 12TH JUNE

Hard Rock Calling
24TH – 26TH JUNE

**Somerset House
Summer Series**
7TH – 17TH JULY

T in the Park
8TH – 10TH JULY

V Festival
20TH – 21ST AUGUST

**Reading & Leeds
Festival**
26TH – 28TH AUGUST

Bestival
8TH – 11TH SEPTEMBER

A TABLE BOOKING

*LadyBlonde.com offers a fast and reliable online
table booking service, so you can find what you're
looking for and book it within a few easy clicks.*

Fully booked? If you're an **LB2B Member** of
LadyBlonde.com there might be something we
can do...

A PARTY OR AN EVENT

If you're planning a party or event – for any occasion, on any scale and within any budget – Lady Blonde's team can help you every step of the way.

From sourcing venues to recommending suppliers, your **LB2B Account Manager** can utilise a wealth of contacts and unrivalled industry knowledge to help you confidently create spectacular parties and events.

HOSPITALITY AT SPORTING EVENTS

Bond with clients whilst experiencing the finest hospitality sourced by LadyBlonde.com.

Rugby at Twickenham
FROM 21ST MAY

Cricket at Lord's
FROM 3RD JUNE

AEGON Championships
6TH – 12TH JUNE

Wimbledon
20TH JUNE – 3RD JULY

British Grand Prix
8TH 10TH JULY

The Open
10TH – 17TH JULY

ATP World Tour
20TH – 27TH NOVEMBER

AEGON Masters
30TH NOV – 4TH DECEMBER

LORD'S

WHISKY MIST

MY DIARY

Keep up to date with the hottest launches, parties and events, by scanning the QR code below or visiting: LadyBlonde.com/events to browse The Diary online and sync it with your own.

See page 7 for full instructions on scanning QR codes.

A BIG NIGHT OUT

Marking a special occasion? Entertaining clients from abroad? If you want to create a night to remember, your LB2B Account Manager will be happy to help.

From making recommendations and reservations to organising transport and accommodation, Lady Blonde's team has it covered with no request too small, no quest too large, and no ideas too off-the-wall or in-demand.

THEATRE OR CONCERT TICKETS

Desperately want to see a particular musical? Your all-time favourite opera? Or (dare we say it) the biggest boy band of all time? Tickets sold out?

We know all the right people and know just where to look, so if there's a ticket you want, we might just be able to help you find it.

I want to find a **VENUE** that is good for...

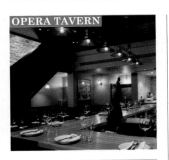

OPERA TAVERN

A DATE

There are enough daunting dating variables to worry about; ensure the location is a sure-fire winner.

CLIENT ENTERTAINING

Whether you want to impress or reward, bond or catch up, each of these destinations will keep clients keen.

SCOTT'S

PIZZA EAST

GROUPS

The bill-splitting pain might remain unavoidable, but at least the booking part can be hassle free.

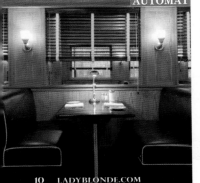

AUTOMAT

BREAKFAST & BRUNCH

It's the most important meal of the day. And – regardless of whether it's for business or pleasure – it can also be the best.

GOING OUT

PRE & POST THEATRE DINING

To make the occasion special, or just to avoid an embarrassing tummy rumble mid-soliloquy, dine early or late and enjoy access to reputably hard-to-get-into restaurants.

LE CAPRICE

VISTA

DESTINATION DRINKS

If you're looking to impress or experience something special, these bars all offer something unique.

Continued on the next page...

Continued from the previous page...

AFTERNOON TEA

Quintessentially British, it's no surprise that London offers the best afternoon teas in the world.

BROWN'S HOTEL

FOODIES

With some of the world's finest chefs working in the Capital, London is a culinary playground for foodies.

AT BAR DINING

Counter-dining is a relaxed (and sometimes interactive) way to enjoy some of London's top restaurants.

SHARER PLATES

Sometimes three courses offer too much food and formality and not enough variety; share, and less becomes more.

GALVIN AT WINDOWS

OUT OF TOWNERS

Restaurants and bars that showcase the best of British, a London view or something unique, are experiences an out-of-towner should enjoy (it's not showing off, it's sharing).

MIN JIANG

COFFEE CATCH-UPS? AFTER WORK DRINKS? SPEAKEASY BARS?

For further venue recommendations, simply scan the QR code on the right with your phone or visit LadyBlonde.com/favourites to read Lady Blonde's Favourites articles online.

For full instructions on using QR codes, see page 7.

I want to find a **VENUE** with...

ALTITUDE LONDON

WOW FACTOR

*Big and beautiful,
flash and showy or
unexpectedly impressive,
wow factor makes an
event unforgettable.*

A PRIVATE DINING ROOM

*Planning an intimate
occasion or an important
meeting? These private
dining rooms all have
something special to offer.*

MEWS OF MAYFAIR

MOVIDA

A DANCE FLOOR

*No party is complete
without dancing (on the
tables). These nightclubs
are all available for
private hire.*

CLARIDGE'S

A TRADITIONAL SPACE OR BALLROOM

*For traditional weddings and grand occasions,
large-scale quintessentially British locations
will deliver.*

SOMETHING INTERACTIVE

Offering your guests interactive experiences is a sure-fire way to keep a party fun, an event memorable, and a day out rewarding.

BISLEY SHOOTING

AN ALFRESCO SPACE

For Summer soirées or Winter wonderlands, parties outside offer something unique and impressive.

A SCREENING ROOM

For premieres, presentations and parties, London's best screening rooms range from hi-tech to lavish.

A BLANK CANVAS SPACE

Require a blank backdrop or elaborate room transformation? Creativity can run freely in these versatile spaces.

SANCTUM SOHO HOTEL

A CHEF'S TABLE? BIG CAPACITY?

Scan the QR code or visit LadyBlonde.com for more venue recommendations.

For full instructions on using QR codes, see page 7.

I want to find a **VENUE** to host...

CLARIDGE'S

A WEDDING

From the grand to the intimate, these venues excel at delivering exceptional weddings.

A BRAINSTORM

Planning a small meeting? A large conference? It's pens-at-the-ready in these well-appointed venues.

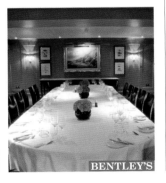

BENTLEY'S

KOSMOPOL

BIRTHDAY PARTY

If you're celebrating a birthday, these venues are perfect for combining drinks, music and friends.

THE BREWERY

A LAUNCH PARTY OR FASHION SHOW

From the trusted to the unexpected, these spaces are all brandable and the settings are all memorable.

AN EXTRAVAGANZA

Planning an event with more razzmatazz than a sea of jazz hands? These venues cater for large-scale spectacular parties, brimming with wow factor.

INDIGO2

A CHRISTMAS PARTY

Christmas parties call for atmospheric spaces, opulent finishes and late night licenses.

A SUMMER PARTY

The Riviera is all very well, but there is no better backdrop to a party than a sunny London.

A COCKTAIL PARTY

Keep them chic and glamorous and full of style for a cocktail party to remember.

CAFÉ DE PARIS

A CHILDREN'S PARTY?

Scan the QR code or visit LadyBlonde.com for more venue recommendations.

For full instructions on using QR codes, see page 7.

I am hosting an event and need help with...

ORGANISING, PLANNING & PRODUCTION
I want to find people who are good for...

NIEMIERKO

PLANNING WEDDINGS

On a day when perfection is paramount, bring in an expert to ensure every delicate detail is delivered.

CHILDREN'S PARTIES

Apparently pass-the-parcel isn't enough anymore; parties for children and families require a magical touch.

TIKES & TIARAS

SNOOK EVENTS

BIRTHDAY PARTIES

Milestone birthdays are not to be feared; the older you get, the better parties you can throw.

QUINTESSENTIALLY EVENTS

PARTY EXTRAVAGANZAS

If you're going all out, you can't miss anything out – bring in a pro to deliver a visual and veritable feast.

LIGHTING, SOUND, DRESSING & PRODUCTION

From elaborate theming to jaw-dropping light shows, nothing is beyond the realms of possibility.

THEME TRADERS

STRATEGIC CORPORATE EVENTS

Everyone loves a good party, but how do you ensure your corporate events deliver reward and return?

HIGH SOCIETY

EVENT STAFF

Don't let your guests be offered a "can-ayp"; the right staff is the key to a great event.

AURA

KEEPING UP WITH LATEST TRENDS IN ORGANISING EVENTS

For the latest tips, trends and ideas for planning parties and events, simply scan the QR code or visit LadyBlonde.com to read Lady Blonde's dedicated articles online.

For full instructions on using QR codes, see page 7.

I am hosting an event and need help with...

FOOD & DRINK
I want to find people who are good for...

PICNIC2U

LUXURY CAR PARK PICNICS

Whether you're entertaining clients or just keeping up with the Joneses, the perfect car park picnic at a social or sporting event is the ultimate luxury and a guaranteed status-maker.

Archie's At Home	P.108
deWintons	P.110
Melon	P.104
Picnic2U	P.111
True Deli	P.111

CANAPÉ PARTIES

A well-executed canapé party is an art form; consideration is given from how and when the bite-size delicacies are served, to their taste, design, colour and composition.

Admirable Crichton	P.100
Blue Strawberry	P.109
deWintons	P.110
Noble House Events	P.110
True Deli	P.111

DE WINTONS

BERRY SCRUMPTIOUS

MAILABLE TREATS

Want to say thank you, congratulations or sorry? Want to send unique invitations? A delicious treat through a letterbox is the sweetest way.

Berry Scrumptious	P.109
Doughdough.com	P.110
Fortnum & Mason	P.115
Gift-Library.com	P.115
Happy Box London	P.116

AT HOME DINNER PARTIES

Sometimes a restaurant is too much, while entertaining at home is stressful and messy. But turn to these top caterers and they'll leave without a trace, and without breaking the bank (or your finest china).

DELIVERANCE

URBAN CAPRICE

LARGE SCALE PARTIES

Catering for large numbers can cause concern over quality and consistency, but these exceptional caterers can deliver top-quality food on every scale.

WEDDING BANQUETS

The first meal with your new spouse is symbolically important, so you want it to be perfect for you, your family and your guests. It's also handy for mopping up Champagne.

KEEPING UP WITH THE LATEST TRENDS IN FOOD, DRINK & EVENT CATERING

For further venue recommendations, simply scan the QR code or visit LadyBlonde.com/favourites to read Lady Blonde's Favourites articles online.

For full instructions on using QR codes, see page 7.

I am hosting an event and need help with...

ENTERTAINMENT
I want to find people who are good for...

TIKES & TIARAS

ADDING SOMETHING EXTRA

It's the little things that add up to a spectacular event. If you're looking for entertainment, or unique additions to complement your party, look no further.

CHILDREN'S ENTERTAINMENT

To offer "the fairytale party of your dreams" to an adult is gallingly clichéd. But for a child, the right party really is a dream come true.

NOTORIOUS PRODUCTIONS

GENIE FILM

CREATING EXPERIENCES

Looking to do something different to mark an occasion? Witness a sporting clash; go on an outdoor adventure; star in your own James Bond movie: the sky's the limit.

I am hosting an event and need help with...

THE FINISHING TOUCHES
I want to find people who are good for...

PICCOLO PRESS

STATIONERY & CALLIGRAPHY

First impressions are everything, and as everything starts with an invitation, make sure yours are the best your money can buy.

Mount Street Printers	P.116
Paul Antonio Scribe	P.116
Piccolo Press	P.117
Walton Street Stationery	P.118
Wren Press	P.118

FLORAL ARRANGEMENTS

Flowers don't just complement an event; they can add a whole new dimension, integrating style, aroma, colour and design.

Birksen	P.115
Moyses Stevens	P.116
Robbie Honey	P.117
Rob Van Helden	P.117
Sophie Hanna	P.117

ROB VAN HELDEN

TRUE DELI

CORPORATE GIFTING

Whether it's something traditional or unique, thoughtful or flash, off-the-peg or personalised, the right gift is worth every penny.

Doughdough.com	P.110
Fortnum & Mason	P.115
Gift-Library.com	P.115
Happy Box London	P.116
U'luvka	P.118

I am attending an event and need help with...

GETTING THE LOOK
I want to find people who are good for...

PRE PARTY
PREP & PAMPERING

*Don't be outshone by your centerpieces.
A pre-party blow-dry is as crucial as
remembering to put your clothes on.*

Brooks & Brooks	P.119
The Chapel	P.119
Daniel Galvin	P.120
Daniel Hersheson	P.120
Hari's	P.121
John Frieda	P.121
Kell Skött Haircare	P.121
Paul Edmonds	P.122
Philip Kingsley	P.122
Taylor Taylor London	P.122

THE CHAPEL

MANDARIN ORIENTAL

A SPA DAY

*Whether it's to look the part for an event,
or to wind down afterwards, if you can
think of an excuse to visit one of
London's luxurious spas, do.*

Agua Spa	P.119
BeautyWorksWest	P.119
Cowshed	P.120
Gentlemen's Tonic	P.120
Mandarin Oriental	P.122

KEEPING UP WITH THE LATEST
TRENDS IN PRE PARTY PREENING

*For the latest tips, trends and ideas in getting the
look, simply scan the QR code with your phone or visit
LadyBlonde.com/favourites to read Lady Blonde's
dedicated articles online.*

For full instructions on using QR codes, see page 7.

I want to dine out *and...*
STAY IN SHAPE

We work hard. We play hard. Our health suffers.
So, *LadyBlonde.com* has teamed up with **LOMAX Bespoke Health** to help
Londoners maintain a healthy balance (for contact details see pg. 121).

NUTRITION

LOMAX *designs realistic eating plans to help with fat loss, energy levels, sleeping patterns and general health.*

IN YOUR HOME
Benefit from an inexpensive food delivery service, including all meals, drinks and snacks.

IN THEIR SPACE
Enjoy bespoke food boxes designed by expert nutritionists in the healthy food café.

PERSONAL TRAINING

LOMAX *offers highly trained personal trainers utilising many different fitness methods.*

IN YOUR HOME
Get fit at a time and place that suits you with **LOMAX Personal Trainers.**

IN THEIR SPACE
LOMAX Victoria offers a state-of-the-art **'PODULAR'** fitness space with a vast array of low-cost training options.

WELLBEING

LOMAX *focuses on all systems of the body – from immune to reproductive – to achieve total wellbeing.*

IN YOUR HOME
Benefit from consultations, massage, complementary medicine, and more in a place to suit you.

IN THEIR SPACE
Stay in peak condition with specialist on-site treatments at **LOMAX Victoria**.

MENU ANALYSIS

Allergies? Intolerances? Weight-loss goals or training regimes to adhere to? For some people, eating out can be more of a pain than a pleasure. But not anymore.

LOMAX offers a free, personalised online **Menu Analysis** service for every restaurant on **LadyBlonde.com**, with one simple click.

GALLERY OF VENUES

ALTITUDE LONDON

VENUES

London – home to world-renowned chefs and spectacular entertainment, and awash with stunning architecture, intriguing spaces and trend-setting interior designers – has a setting to suit every occasion.

From the impressive and unique through to the intimate and cosy, you'll find what you're looking for here.

30 PAVILION ROAD
AN EVENT SPACE

"A Georgian Town House in the heart of Knightsbridge? A luxurious gem that one should try and claim is one's own."

30 Pavilion Road, London SW1X 0HJ
T: *020 7823 9212* W: *www.30pavilionroad.co.uk*

OPENING HOURS:
Sunday to Wednesday
8am – 12am
Thursday to Saturday
8am – 1am

GOOD FOR HOSTING...
...an elegant cocktail reception in **The Stone Hall** with an open fire for up to 240 people.
...an intimate dinner in the antique wood-paneled **Library**.
...a chic and elegant wedding, with a sumptuous banquet followed by dancing in **The Ballroom**.
...a conference with clients and colleagues with break-out rooms, seminars and a sit down dinner to finish.

LOCATION: Knightsbridge
NEAREST TUBE: Knightsbridge
FUNCTION ROOMS: 3
CAPACITY: 120 seated / 240 standing
PRIVATE DINING: 26, 120
CIVIL CEREMONIES: Yes
CUISINE: British

40|30 AT THE GHERKIN
A PRIVATE MEMBERS' CLUB

"40|30 is the restaurant and bar at the very top of the Gherkin - one of the most iconic buildings in London. So if you're looking to impress, you know what they say: big building, big... party."

30 St Mary Axe, London EC3A 8EP
T: *020 7071 5009* W: *www.searcys.co.uk/40-30-the-gherkin*

OPENING HOURS:
Open daily for members and private hire

GOOD FOR GOING OUT...
...if you're lucky enough to be a member, or work in the building.

GOOD FOR HOSTING...
...a working lunch in a private dining room with spectacular views over London.
...a Champagne and canapé reception with wow factor and a contemporary feel, under the glass dome that offers 360 degree, panoramic views.
...a wedding with an exquisite dinner in the restaurant for up to 90 people, followed by dancing in the mezzanine bar.

LOCATION: The City
NEAREST TUBE: Aldgate
FUNCTION ROOMS: 3
CAPACITY: 90 seated / 260 standing
PRIVATE DINING: 12, 15, 90
CIVIL CEREMONIES: Yes
CUISINE: French

ADAM STREET
A PRIVATE MEMBERS' CLUB

"An atmospheric and unique vaulted members' club below The Strand, Adam Street draws a crowd who party as hard as they work."

9 Adam Street, London WC2N 6AA
T: *020 7379 8000* W: *www.adamstreet.co.uk*

OPENING HOURS:
Monday to Wednesday / Thursday / Friday
8:30am –1am / 8:30am – 2am / 8:30am – 3am
Saturday
6pm – 3am

GOOD FOR GOING OUT...
...if you're lucky enough to be a member.

GOOD FOR HOSTING...
...a low-key launch party or exhibition in ***The Gallery*** for an entrepreneurial crowd.
...a fun and relaxed Christmas cocktail party with colleagues, with fully inclusive packages.
...a birthday party with Champagne and canapés, and dancing with friends until the early hours.

LOCATION: Embankment
NEAREST TUBE: Charing Cross
FUNCTION ROOMS: 5
CAPACITY: 80 seated / 350 standing
PRIVATE DINING: 12, 60, 80
CIVIL CEREMONIES: Yes
CUISINE: British

ALL STAR LANES
BOWLING ALLEY

"No need to endure warm pints and fast food here: All Star Lanes combines cocktails, indulgent diner food and a fun bowling atmosphere."

6 Porchester Gardens, London W2 4DB
T: *020 7313 8363* W: *www.allstarlanes.co.uk*

OPENING HOURS:
Monday to Thursday
4pm – 11:30pm
Friday / Saturday / Sunday
12pm – 12am / 11am – 12am / 11am – 10:30pm

GOOD FOR GOING OUT...
...on a relaxed and fun first date.
...on a night out with friends looking to do something different.
...with a bowling enthusiast.

GOOD FOR HOSTING...
...a fun and active party with friends in the private room, with your own cocktail bar and two bowling lanes.
...a relaxed team-building activity with colleagues and clients.

LOCATION: Bayswater
NEAREST TUBE: Bayswater
FUNCTION ROOMS: 2
CAPACITY: 350 standing
PRIVATE DINING: N/A
CIVIL CEREMONIES: No
CUISINE: American

ALMADA
A PRIVATE MEMBERS' CLUB

"A discreet private members' club with an unmarked door, Almada is a decadent hideaway for the glamorous Mayfair set."

17 Berkeley Street, Mayfair, London W1J 8EA
T: *020 7290 4500*

OPENING HOURS:
Thursday - Saturday
8pm – 3am

GOOD FOR GOING OUT...
...if you're lucky enough to be a member.

GOOD FOR HOSTING...
...a private dinner with a jet-set crowd, in a relaxed but refined setting.
...a hedonistic Christmas cocktail party with chic and fashionable friends.
...a launch party with effortless style.
...an art exhibition in an atmospheric, stylish setting.

LOCATION: Mayfair
NEAREST TUBE: Green Park
FUNCTION ROOMS: 2
CAPACITY: 155 seated / 200 standing
PRIVATE DINING: 155
CIVIL CEREMONIES: No
CUISINE: Modern European

REVIEW ONLINE

ALTITUDE LONDON
EVENT SPACE & PRIVATE MEMBERS' CLUB

"The views from this riverside tower are breath-taking; Altitude offers a natural high."

21-24 Millbank, London SW1P 4QP
T: *0845 500 3500* W: *www.altitudelondon.com*

OPENING HOURS:
Open daily
7am – 2am

GOOD FOR GOING OUT...
...to **The London Sky Bar** if you are a member, or a non-member with persuasive skills to sweet-talk the doorman.
...on a date to enjoy cocktails, a wonderful view and to do something a bit different.
...for cocktails with a group of people from out of town.

GOOD FOR HOSTING...
...an impressive event for up to 1,200 people in a contemporary, sleek and glossy setting.
...a corporate event with a need for multimedia equipment and branding opportunities.
...a screening or presentation for up to 300 people.

LOCATION: Westminster
NEAREST TUBE: Pimlico
FUNCTION ROOMS: 7
CAPACITY: 400 seated / 1,200 standing
PRIVATE DINING: 80, 95, 240, 400
CIVIL CEREMONIES: Yes
CUISINE: British

AMIKA
A BAR & NIGHTCLUB

"Tucked away under Kensington High Street, Amika offers three sleek spaces to cater for all moods."

65 High Street Kensington, London W8 5ED
T: *020 7850 0419* W: *www.amikalondon.com*

OPENING HOURS:
Thursday to Saturday
10pm – 4am

GOOD FOR GOING OUT...
...on a night out for cocktails and dancing with friends.
...with a group of girls who want to chat as well as dance the night away.
...for members who want to enjoy the luxury of the **Champagne Lounge**.

GOOD FOR HOSTING...
...an atmospheric event during the day.
...an early evening cocktail party to network with clients.
...a launch party or fashion show for a fashionable crowd.

LOCATION: Kensington
NEAREST TUBE: High St Kensington
FUNCTION ROOMS: 4
CAPACITY: 600 standing
PRIVATE DINING: N/A
CIVIL CEREMONIES: No
CUISINE: N/A

AQUA KYOTO
A RESTAURANT & BAR

"With a buzzing bar (aqua spirit) and a roof terrace with table service and heaters, aqua kyoto is a great destination for drinks and dinner."

240 Regent Street, London W1 3BR (Entrance 30 Argyll Street)
T: *020 7478 0540* W: *www.aqua-london.com*

OPENING HOURS:
Monday to Wednesday / Thursday to Saturday
12pm – 3pm; 6pm –11pm / 11:30pm

GOOD FOR GOING OUT...
...for after-work drinks with colleagues and clients to somewhere buzzy and sophisticated.
...with someone from out of town who loves Japanese food.
...for drinks and dinner with a glamorous date.
...for a walk-in lunch on the alfresco terrace (Summer only).

GOOD FOR HOSTING...
...a decadent lunch with clients in a sophisticated private dining room.
...a special dinner fueled by cocktails with friends in a private dining room.

LOCATION: West End
NEAREST TUBE: Oxford Circus
FUNCTION ROOMS: 3
CAPACITY: 110 seated / 200 standing
PRIVATE DINING: 10, 110
CIVIL CEREMONIES: Yes
CUISINE: Japanese

THE ARCH LONDON
A HOTEL

"Situated in a quiet spot behind Marble Arch, this intimate five star hotel offers stylish and discreet surroundings."

50 Great Cumberland Place, London W1H 7FD
T: *020 7724 4700* W: *www.thearchlondon.com*

GOOD FOR GOING OUT...
...for a quiet working lunch with colleagues.
...when you want to escape the crowds of Oxford Street at any time of day.
...to sample great cocktails in the discreet ***Champagne Bar***.

GOOD FOR HOSTING...
...a birthday party with friends in the ***Martini Library***.
...a refined but low-key drinks party to network with colleagues and clients.
...a boardroom meeting, in comfortable style, for up to 20 people.

LOCATION: Marble Arch
NEAREST TUBE: Marble Arch
FUNCTION ROOMS: 3
CAPACITY: 40 seated / 50 standing
PRIVATE DINING: 10, 18, 30
CIVIL CEREMONIES: No
CUISINE: Modern European

THE ATTIC
A BAR

"With decadent decor and breathtaking views, The Attic is a unique offering making the trip to Canary Wharf (and the ride to the 48th floor) worth all the effort."

48th Floor, 3 Pan Peninsula Square, London E14 9HN
T: *020 8305 3091* W: *www.incgroup.co.uk*

OPENING HOURS:
Friday and Saturday / Monday to Thursday
5pm – 12am / By appointment only

GOOD FOR GOING OUT...
...for delicious cocktails in a unique and impressive setting with a date.
...for after-work drinks to relax and be inspired by the panoramic views over the whole city, the river Thames and the futuristic skyline of Canary Wharf.

GOOD FOR HOSTING...
...a cocktail party with wow factor and a 1950s glamorous feel, in a unique location for up to 80 guests.

LOCATION: Canary Wharf
NEAREST TUBE: South Quays DLR
FUNCTION ROOMS: 1
CAPACITY: 80 standing
PRIVATE DINING: N/A
CIVIL CEREMONIES: No
CUISINE: Canapés

AUTOMAT
A RESTAURANT

"Automat is an ideal location for those with substantial appetites for both American fare and the social scene."

33 Dover Street, London W1S 4NF
T: *020 7499 3033* W: *www.automat-london.com*

OPENING HOURS:
Monday to Friday
7am – 12am
Saturday and Sunday
10am – 12am / 10pm

GOOD FOR GOING OUT...
...with a lively group of friends to enjoy authentic American diner food.
...for lunch with a group of guys to discuss business and boy stuff.
...for a delicious and indulgent breakfast or brunch.

GOOD FOR HOSTING...
...a buzzy birthday dinner for up to 12 people at the chef's table.

LOCATION: Mayfair
NEAREST TUBE: Green Park
FUNCTION ROOMS: N/A
CAPACITY: N/A
PRIVATE DINING: N/A
CIVIL CEREMONIES: No
CUISINE: American

BALTIC
A RESTAURANT

"As is the Eastern European custom, it is strongly advised to follow every course with at least one shot of vodka. I know – it's such a bind."

74 Blackfriars Road, London SE1 8HA
T: *020 7928 1111* W: *www.balticrestaurant.co.uk*

OPENING HOURS:
Open Daily
Restaurant: 12pm – 3:30pm; 5:30pm – 11:15pm
Bar: 12pm – 12am

GOOD FOR GOING OUT...
...on a date when vodka is needed to calm nerves.
...for cocktails in the **Amber Bar** before a fun dinner
    with friends.
...for a relaxed lunch with colleagues.
...for dinner with clients whom you want to make friends with.

GOOD FOR HOSTING...
...a low key and discreet dinner for up to 30 people in the
    private dining room, looking over the impressive space.
...a seated event for 150 people with a DJ and live music.

LOCATION: Southwark
NEAREST TUBE: Southwark
FUNCTION ROOMS: 2
CAPACITY: 150 seated / 400 standing
PRIVATE DINING: 33, 150
CIVIL CEREMONIES: No
CUISINE: Eastern European

BARRAFINA
A RESTAURANT & BAR

"This tapas bar always delivers great food and service – a great date place."

54 Frith Street, London W1D 4SL
T: *020 7813 8016* W: *www.barrafina.co.uk*

OPENING HOURS:
Monday to Saturday
12pm – 3pm; 5pm – 11pm
Sunday
1pm – 3:30pm; 5:30pm – 10pm

GOOD FOR GOING OUT...
...for dinner when you are not in a hurry as reservations
    are not accepted.
...on a relaxed first date to share small plates and drink
    delicious wine in a bustling Soho hotspot.
...for a catch up with a girlfriend.
...with a lover of exceptional Spanish tapas.

LOCATION: Soho
NEAREST TUBE: Tottenham Court Rd
FUNCTION ROOMS: N/A
CAPACITY: N/A
PRIVATE DINING: N/A
CIVIL CEREMONIES: No
CUISINE: Tapas

LOCATION: Chelsea
NEAREST TUBE: Sloane Square
FUNCTION ROOMS: 1
CAPACITY: 50 seated / 80 standing
PRIVATE DINING: 50
CIVIL CEREMONIES: Yes
CUISINE: N/A

BARTS
A BAR

"A quirky speakeasy-style bar with a Cuban-themed Havana garden, on Sloane Avenue."

Sloane Avenue, London SW3 3DW
T: *020 7581 3355* W: *www.barts-london.com*

OPENING HOURS:
Monday to Thursday / Friday and Saturday / Sunday
6pm – 12:30am / 6pm – 1:30am / 6pm – 11pm

GOOD FOR GOING OUT…
…for cocktails with friends in a fun and funky setting.
…for a night of drinking, dressing up and carefree abandon.
…and impressing a date, by gaining entry to the bar through the hidden door.

GOOD FOR HOSTING…
…an early evening cocktail party for up to 80 people, with a fun and celebratory feel.
…a quirkily-themed party that encourages dressing up and guarantees a hangover.

LOCATION: The City
NEAREST TUBE: Liverpool Street
FUNCTION ROOMS: 2
CAPACITY: 120 seated / 220 standing
PRIVATE DINING: 120
CIVIL CEREMONIES: No
CUISINE: Modern European

THE BATHHOUSE
A RESTAURANT, BAR & LIVE ENTERTAINMENT VENUE

"Originally a Victorian Bathhouse, this opulent City hideaway has been restored to its former glory and serves delicious cocktails and food to a backdrop of intriguing entertainment."

7-8 Bishopsgate Churchyard, London EC2M 3TJ
T: *020 7920 9207* W: *www.thebathhousevenue.com*

OPENING HOURS:
Thursday / Friday / Saturday
5pm – 12am / 5pm – 4am / 8pm – 4am

GOOD FOR GOING OUT…
…for a date with a difference.
…for a client dinner with an edge.
…for dinner and entertainment with a group of fun friends.
…for late night cocktails to unleash your inner iniquity.

GOOD FOR HOSTING…
…a sparkling birthday soiree with a banquet-style feast.
…an evening of cocktails with colleagues in a semi-private booth.
…a festive corporate Christmas party.

BATTERY CLUB
A PRIVATE MEMBERS' CLUB

"Canary Wharf's first members' club, Battery Club offers breathtaking views of the Thames and the City from a stunning glass lighthouse-style building designed by Philippe Starck."

34 Westferry Circus, London E14 8RR
T: *020 8305 3089* W: *www.thebatteryclub.co.uk*

OPENING HOURS:
Open daily for members and private hire

GOOD FOR GOING OUT...
...if you're lucky enough to be a member.

GOOD FOR HOSTING...
...a sunset cocktail reception with breathtaking views across the City.
...a fun birthday party with live music and late night dancing to a DJ.
...a relaxed business drinks party in a stylish setting with a chic long bar and New York vibe.
...a funky weekend wedding.

LOCATION: Canary Wharf
NEAREST TUBE: Canary Wharf
FUNCTION ROOMS: 2
CAPACITY: 200 seated / 220 standing
PRIVATE DINING: N/A
CIVIL CEREMONIES: Yes
CUISINE: Modern European

BEAUFORT HOUSE
A PRIVATE MEMBERS' CLUB

"Set over 3 floors, Beaufort House is a stylish Champagne bar, restaurant and members' club."

354 Kings Road, London SW3 5UZ
T: *020 7352 2828* W: *www.beauforthousechelsea.co.uk*

OPENING HOURS:
Sunday to Tuesday / Wednesday and Thursday
9am – 1:30am / 9am – 2:30am
Friday and Saturday
9am – 3:30am

GOOD FOR GOING OUT...
...for a light lunch with a girlfriend.
...for delicious cocktails in the buzzy ground floor bar.
...with a member who can sneak you upstairs for late night dining.

GOOD FOR HOSTING...
...a board meeting and private screening on the 63" HD plasma.
...a birthday party in the stylishly designed Champagne bar for glamorous friends.
...a chic private dinner and reception drinks with friends.

LOCATION: Chelsea
NEAREST TUBE: Sloane Square
FUNCTION ROOMS: 3
CAPACITY: 150 seated / 150 standing
PRIVATE DINING: 22, 100, 150
CIVIL CEREMONIES: Yes
CUISINE: Modern European

The Jameson Room

LOCATION: Mayfair
NEAREST TUBE: Piccadilly Circus
FUNCTION ROOMS: 2
CAPACITY: 60 seated / 100 standing
PRIVATE DINING: 14, 60
CIVIL CEREMONIES: No
CUISINE: Seafood

BENTLEY'S OYSTER BAR & GRILL
A RESTAURANT & BAR

"Despite the Mayfair location, Bentley's is a relaxed place to enjoy delicious seafood."

11-15 Swallow Street, London W1B 4DG
T: *020 7734 4756* W: *www.bentleysoysterbarandgrill.co.uk*

OPENING HOURS:
Monday to Friday
Oyster Bar: 7am – 11am; *The Grill:* 12pm – 3pm; 6pm –11pm
Saturday / Sunday
Oyster Bar: 12pm – 12am / 12pm – 10pm
The Grill: Closed / 12pm – 3pm; 6pm – 11pm / 6pm – 10pm

GOOD FOR GOING OUT...
...for a relaxed date, counter-dining on Champagne and oysters.
...for an alfresco lunch in the Summer months.
...for a refined lunch with clients in the first floor restaurant.
...for dinner with relaxed but traditional parents.

GOOD FOR HOSTING...
...an elegant working lunch for up to 14 guests.
...a canapé reception and seated dinner for 100 guests
    followed by dancing until 3am in the ***Jameson Room***.

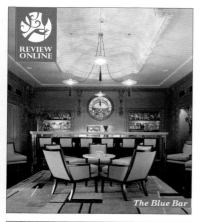

The Blue Bar

LOCATION: Knightsbridge
NEAREST TUBE: Hyde Park Corner
FUNCTION ROOMS: 6
CAPACITY: 200 seated / 400 standing
PRIVATE DINING: 10, 14, 18, 20, 200
CIVIL CEREMONIES: Yes
CUISINE: Afternoon Tea, French

THE BERKELEY
A HOTEL

"The elegant, five star Berkeley benefits from two exceptional restaurants (Marcus Wareing at The Berkeley and Koffmann's), the Blue Bar, a fabulous spa and more."

Wilton Place, London SW1X 7RL
T: *020 7235 6000* W: *www.the-berkeley.co.uk*

GOOD FOR GOING OUT...
...with a glamorous date for cocktails at a pre-booked table
    at the chic ***Blue Bar***.
...to celebrate a special occasion at ***Marcus Wareing at
    The Berkeley*** with your husband or wife.
...for a client lunch at sophisticated ***Koffmann's*** with a
    lover of French cuisine.
...for a quirky afternoon tea for a luxurious girls day out.

GOOD FOR HOSTING...
...a traditional wedding under elegant glass chandeliers.
...an intimate dinner in one of the 6 stylish and traditional
    private dining rooms.
...a lavish launch party in ***The Ballroom***.

THE BIG EASY
A RESTAURANT & LIVE ENTERTAINMENT VENUE

"Cocktails, surf 'n' turf, live music and a fun-loving crowd; your nights will be big and the vibe will be easy."

332-334 Kings Road, London SW3 5UR
T: *020 7352 4071* W: *www.bigeasy.uk.com*

OPENING HOURS:
Monday to Thursday / Friday and Saturday / Sunday
12pm – 11pm / 12pm – 11:30pm / 12pm – 10:30pm

GOOD FOR GOING OUT...
...for after-work drinks with friends to unwind.
...for a relaxed and cocktail-fueled date with someone fun.
...for dinner with a group of friends who like a good sing-song and to get stuck into their food.

GOOD FOR HOSTING...
...a birthday dinner with a raucous group of friends to a backdrop of live music.

LOCATION: Chelsea
NEAREST TUBE: South Kensington
FUNCTION ROOMS: 1
CAPACITY: 162 seated
PRIVATE DINING: N/A
CIVIL CEREMONIES: No
CUISINE: American / Steak / Seafood

BISLEY SHOOTING GROUND
A SHOOTING GROUND

"A day shooting clays at Bisley Shooting Ground combines wonderful service, excellent tuition and a relaxed setting with a competitive and seriously fun activity."

Bisley Camp, Brookwood, Woking, Surrey GU24 ONY
T: *01483 797 017* W: *www.bisleyshooting.co.uk*

OPENING HOURS:
Open daily
9am – 4pm

GOOD FOR GOING OUT...
...for a fun day with friends to do something different and brush up on your shooting skills.
...with a group of clients to bond in a relaxed, rewarding and enjoyable setting.

GOOD FOR HOSTING...
...a unique and hugely enjoyable corporate day out for groups of 10 – 300 people.
...a delicious lunch followed by a shooting competition and drinks reception.

REVIEW ONLINE

LOCATION: Surrey
NEAREST STATION: Brookwood
FUNCTION ROOMS: 3
CAPACITY: 300 standing
PRIVATE DINING: N/A
CIVIL CEREMONIES: No
CUISINE: British

THE BLUES KITCHEN
A BAR & LIVE ENTERTAINMENT VENUE

"This Blues bar offers a chilled but lively hub in Camden, where locals enjoy American cuisine and live music."

---

111 Camden High Street, London NW1 7JN
T: *020 7387 5277* W: *www.theblueskitchen.com*

OPENING HOURS:
Monday to Wednesday / Thursday / Friday
12pm – 12am / 12pm – 1am / 12pm – 3am

GOOD FOR GOING OUT...
...for some no frills American food with a group of friends to dance to some Rhythm and Blues.
...when you want to sit in a booth, drink cocktails and graze on food with friends.

GOOD FOR HOSTING...
...a fun birthday party with a mixed group when you want to drink, dance and dally with Blues.
...an informal Christmas party with colleagues who don't like anything flash.
...a party in the whole venue with live performances.

LOCATION: Camden
NEAREST TUBE: Camden Town
FUNCTION ROOMS: 1
CAPACITY: 150 seated / 300 standing
PRIVATE DINING: N/A
CIVIL CEREMONIES: No
CUISINE: American

BOCCA DI LUPO
A RESTAURANT

"Relaxed, refined and with regional cuisine, Bocca di Lupo offers a slice of Italy in the heart of Soho."

---

12 Archer Street, London W1D 7BB
T: *020 7734 2223* W: *www.boccadilupo.com*

OPENING HOURS:
Monday to Saturday
12:30pm – 3pm; 5:30pm – 12am
Sunday
12pm – 4pm

GOOD FOR GOING OUT...
...for pre- or post-theatre dinner with a lover of authentic Italian cuisine.
...for a dinner date at the marble-topped bar and enjoying an atmospheric and relaxed evening.
...for an intimate dinner in the effortlessly stylish restaurant with friends.

GOOD FOR HOSTING...
...a relaxed but refined lunch or dinner for 10 – 32 people around one large wooden table in the private dining room.

LOCATION: Soho
NEAREST TUBE: Piccadilly Circus
FUNCTION ROOMS: 2
CAPACITY: 60 seated
PRIVATE DINING: 32, 60
CIVIL CEREMONIES: No
CUISINE: Italian

BOISDALE

A RESTAURANT, BAR & LIVE ENTERTAINMENT VENUE

"Full of tradition and packed with character, Boisdale is an ever-popular haunt for those that like to live a little."

15 Eccleston Street, London SW1W 9LX
T: 020 7730 6922 W: *www.boisdale.co.uk*

OPENING HOURS:
Monday to Friday / Saturday
12pm – 1am / 6pm – 1am

GOOD FOR GOING OUT...
...for drinks under a rug on the *Cigar Terrace* followed by dinner and live jazz with a date.
...for a steak- and wine-orientated lunch with clients.
...for dinner with a group of jazz-lovers.

GOOD FOR HOSTING...
...an alfresco lunch for up to 20 people in the beautifully planted courtyard, in the Summer.
...an alfresco (but heated) candlelit and atmospheric dinner party for up to 20 people all year round.
...drinks for 40 people in the traditional pub-style *Back Bar*.

LOCATION: Belgravia
NEAREST TUBE: Victoria
FUNCTION ROOMS: 2
CAPACITY: 140 seated / 230 standing
PRIVATE DINING: 22, 140
CIVIL CEREMONIES: Yes
CUISINE: British / Steak

BOUNDARY

A HOTEL

"With a bakery, a restaurant, a café, a rooftop terrace and a hotel, Conran has created a masterpiece with no boundaries at all."

2-4 Boundary Street, London E2 7DD
(Entrance in Redchurch Street)
T: 020 7729 1051 W: *www.theboundary.co.uk*

GOOD FOR GOING OUT...
...for a catch up with a friend over a fresh and delicious breakfast at *Albion at Boundary*.
...for an after-work drink-date on *The Rooftop* during the Summer months.
...to *The Rooftop* on a Summer's evening with a group of friends for dinner and drinks (no reservations).

GOOD FOR HOSTING...
...a discreet and indulgent drinks party in one of the Conran-designed suites.
...a client lunch in the private dining area of the restaurant.
...a sophisticated dinner in *Boundary Restaurant* for business or pleasure.

LOCATION: Shoreditch
NEAREST TUBE: Old Street
FUNCTION ROOMS: 2
CAPACITY: 136 seated / 160 standing
PRIVATE DINING: 35, 136
CIVIL CEREMONIES: No
CUISINE: French

THE BREWERY
AN EVENT SPACE

"The space is unique, the service is fantastic, the location is convenient and the name is promising."

Chiswell Street, London EC1Y 4SD
T: *020 7638 8811* W: *www.thebrewery.co.uk*

OPENING HOURS:
Open daily for events and private hire

GOOD FOR HOSTING...
...a dinner-dance with wow factor for up to 750 people in the **Porter Tun**.
...a large-scale and impressive awards ceremony with advanced multimedia and live performances for up to 650 people.

LOCATION: The City
NEAREST TUBE: Moorgate
FUNCTION ROOMS: 6
CAPACITY: 750 seated / 1,000 standing
PRIVATE DINING: N/A
CIVIL CEREMONIES: Yes
CUISINE: Flexible catering

THE BROMPTON CLUB
A PRIVATE MEMBERS' CLUB

"Strictly available for members only, The Brompton Club, with a gentleman's club feel, a Euro crowd and a hedonistic vibe, is a top spot in South Ken."

92 Old Brompton Road, London SW7 5LR
T: *020 7268 5906* W: *www.thebromptonclub.com*

OPENING HOURS:
Tuesday to Friday / Saturday
7pm – 2am / 7pm – 3am

GOOD FOR GOING OUT...
...if you're lucky enough to be a member.

GOOD FOR HOSTING...
...a Christmas party with live entertainment in a sexy and opulent setting.
...an early evening launch party or networking event for a glamorous set.
...a poker tournament for colleagues and clients with a secret club vibe.

LOCATION: South Kensington
NEAREST TUBE: South Kensington
FUNCTION ROOMS: 4
CAPACITY: 100 seated / 350 standing
PRIVATE DINING: 20, 50, 100
CIVIL CEREMONIES: No
CUISINE: Modern European

BROWN'S HOTEL

A HOTEL

"With a bar, spa, restaurant and a delicious traditional Afternoon Tea, Brown's is a home-from-home...though perhaps a touch bigger than most people's homes."

Albemarle Street, London W1S 4BP
T: *020 7493 6020* W: *www.brownshotel.com*

GOOD FOR GOING OUT...

...for a sophisticated after-work drink in the chic **Donovan Bar** to a soundtrack of live jazz.

...for a pre-theatre dinner in **HIX at The Albemarle** with your parents.

...for a cosy and traditional afternoon tea with your family.

GOOD FOR HOSTING...

...a formal private dinner or lunch for important clients in discreet but luxurious surroundings.

...a small, intimate and exquisite wedding with an elegant and traditional vibe.

LOCATION: Mayfair
NEAREST TUBE: Green Park
FUNCTION ROOMS: 6
CAPACITY: 72 seated / 120 standing
PRIVATE DINING: 6, 8, 12, 40, 72
CIVIL CEREMONIES: Yes
CUISINE: British / Afternoon tea

BUEN AYRE

A RESTAURANT

"The restaurant may lack frills and fancies but the exquisite Argentine food leaves you wanting for nothing."

50 Broadway Market, London E8 4QJ
T: *020 7275 9900* W: *www.buenayre.co.uk*

OPENING HOURS:

Monday to Thursday
6pm – 10:30pm
Friday / Saturday and Sunday
12pm – 3pm / 12pm – 3:30pm; 6pm – 10:30pm

GOOD FOR GOING OUT...

...for an informal lunch with male colleagues and clients.

...for dinner with friends when you have a steak craving to satiate, and only the best will do.

...for dinner in a relaxed, rustic and characterful atmosphere.

...with a polo player who misses home.

LOCATION: Hackney
NEAREST TUBE: Bethnal Green
FUNCTION ROOMS: N/A
CAPACITY: 34 seated
PRIVATE DINING: N/A
CIVIL CEREMONIES: No
CUISINE: Steak / South American

LOCATION: The West End
NEAREST TUBE: Piccadilly Circus
FUNCTION ROOMS: 4
CAPACITY: 260 seated / 715 standing
PRIVATE DINING: 260
CIVIL CEREMONIES: Yes
CUISINE: Modern European

CAFÉ DE PARIS
AN EVENT SPACE & LIVE ENTERTAINMENT VENUE

"It's one of those venues that seems to have been around forever, but for very good reason: Café de Paris is an opulent London institution."

3-4 Coventry Street, London W1D 6BL
T: *020 7395 5807* W: *www.cafedeparis.com*

OPENING HOURS:

Friday and Saturday / Sunday to Thursday
7pm – 3am / Available for exclusive private hire

GOOD FOR GOING OUT...
...and hiring the VIP room with friends, colleagues and clients on any Friday or Saturday night.
...for a dinner and a live performance show with friends or visitors to do something a little bit different.

GOOD FOR HOSTING...
...a Christmas party extravaganza with live performances and opulent decor to impress guests.
...a Bar or Bat Mitzvah with wow factor, with the opportunity for a dramatic entrance to ensure an unforgettable day.
...a launch or fashion show with a seated dinner and speeches.

LOCATION: Marylebone
NEAREST TUBE: Baker Street
FUNCTION ROOMS: 1
CAPACITY: 100 seated / 150 standing
PRIVATE DINING: 100
CIVIL CEREMONIES: No
CUISINE: French / Belgian

CAFÉ LUC
A RESTAURANT

"A vibrant, friendly dining room and bar offering a classic brasserie menu."

50 Marylebone High Street, London W1U 5HN
T: *020 7258 9878* W: *www.cafeluc.com*

OPENING HOURS:
Monday to Friday
12pm – 11:30pm
Saturday and Sunday
9am – 11:30pm

GOOD FOR GOING OUT...
...for a business lunch with stylish clients.
...for afternoon tea after a successful shop in Marylebone's boutiques with a fashionista friend.
...for a relaxed date with someone glamorous.
...for weekend brunch with your family in buzzy surroundings.

CARAVAN
A RESTAURANT

"Caravan is a rustic and charming restaurant, bar and roastery serving delicious British cuisine and wonderful coffee."

11-13 Exmouth Market, London EC1R 4QD
T: *020 7833 8115* W: *www.caravanonexmouth.co.uk*

OPENING HOURS:
Monday to Friday / Satuday / Sunday
8am – 11pm; 10am – 11pm; 10am – 4pm

GOOD FOR GOING OUT...
...for a delicious and hearty breakfast in an informal, rustic setting with your girlfriend or boyfriend.
...for a catch up lunch with a friend.
...for a relaxed date to share some small plates from the British menu.
...to dine outside on Exmouth Market in the Summer.

GOOD FOR HOSTING...
...a private dinner with friends overlooking the chefs at work and the gleaming roastery machine.

LOCATION: The City
NEAREST TUBE: Farringdon
FUNCTION ROOMS: 2
CAPACITY: 60 seated / 120 standing
PRIVATE DINING: 12, 60
CIVIL CEREMONIES: No
CUISINE: Modern European

CECCONI'S
A RESTAURANT

"Cecconi's will see you through from a business breakfast to a dashing dinner date."

5A Burlington Gardens, London W1S 3EP
T: *020 7434 1500* W: *www.cecconis.co.uk*

OPENING HOURS:
Monday to Friday
7am – 1am
Saturday / Sunday
8am – 1am / 8am – 12am

GOOD FOR GOING OUT...
...for a business breakfast with a fashionable client.
...for Italian cuisine in elegant and buzzy surroundings.
...for a date with someone sociable and stylish.

LOCATION: Mayfair
NEAREST TUBE: Green Park
FUNCTION ROOMS: 1
CAPACITY: 20 seated
PRIVATE DINING: 20
CIVIL CEREMONIES: No
CUISINE: Italian / Bar snacks

CHINA WHITE
A RESTAURANT, BAR & NIGHTCLUB

"Revamped and relocated and with a relaxed restaurant above the club below, China White remains a popular choice in Fitzrovia."

4 Winsley Street, London W1W 8HF
T: *020 7290 0580* W: *www.chinawhite.com*

OPENING HOURS:
Wednesday
Club: 10pm – 3am
Thursday to Saturday
Club: 10pm – 3am; *Restaurant:* 8pm – 12am

GOOD FOR GOING OUT...
...for dinner with friends before dancing the night away.
...for a night out when you want to dance as well as retreat into a private corner with a date.

GOOD FOR HOSTING...
...an intimate but relaxed birthday party in **The Temple Room** with up to 75 friends.
...a decadent and debauched night in the **VIP Room** to celebrate a launch for up to 70 guests.

LOCATION: Fiztrovia
NEAREST TUBE: Oxford Circus
FUNCTION ROOMS: 4
CAPACITY: 50 seated / 575 standing
PRIVATE DINING: 50
CIVIL CEREMONIES: No
CUISINE: Pan Asian

THE CINNAMON CLUB
A RESTAURANT & BAR

"The Cinnamon Club offers modern Indian cuisine in impressive and sophisticated surroundings."

30 Great Smith Street, London SW1P 3BU
T: *020 7222 2555* W: *www.cinnamonclub.com*

OPENING HOURS:
Monday to Friday
7:30am – 9:30am; 12pm – 2:45pm; 6pm – 10:45pm
Saturday
12pm – 2:45pm; 6pm – 10:45pm

GOOD FOR GOING OUT...
...for a relaxed but refined working lunch with clients.
...for a sophisticated dinner with a lover of Indian cuisine.

GOOD FOR HOSTING...
...a private lunch or dinner with clients on the **Mezzanine** level that overlooks the restaurant and benefits from the buzz of the main room.
...a birthday party with friends in the contemporary cocktail bar with drinks, a DJ and dancing.
...an informal business meeting in **The Library**.

LOCATION: Westminster
NEAREST TUBE: St James's Park
FUNCTION ROOMS: 5
CAPACITY: 220 seated / 500 standing
PRIVATE DINING: 30, 60, 130, 220
CIVIL CEREMONIES: Yes
CUISINE: Indian

CIRCUS
A RESTAURANT & LIVE ENTERTAINMENT VENUE

"The door to Circus is discreet, understated and easily missed, but with live acts performing above, on and around the tables, this is a definite case of don't judge a book by its cover."

27-29 Endell Street, London WC2H 9BA
T: *020 7420 9300* W: *www.circus-london.co.uk*

OPENING HOURS:
Monday to Wednesday / Thursday to Saturday
5:30pm – 12am / 5:30pm – 2am

GOOD FOR GOING OUT...
...for a first date with someone you want to impress and entertain.
...for a birthday dinner with a burlesque twist, with a group of friends, followed by cocktails and dancing in the bar.

GOOD FOR HOSTING...
...a cocktail and canapé party for up to 300 colleagues and clients with live entertainment.
...a quirky fashion show with a seated dinner.

LOCATION: West End
NEAREST TUBE: Covent Garden
FUNCTION ROOMS: 1
CAPACITY: 140 seated / 300 standing
PRIVATE DINING: N/A
CIVIL CEREMONIES: No
CUISINE: Pan Asian

CITY GOLF
AN INDOOR GOLF COURSE

"Using full swing simulators and with the choice of playing over 50 courses, City Golf is a unique place to entertain anyone from beginners to golf-fanatics."

40 Coleman St, London EC2R 5EH
T: *020 7796 5960* W: *www.citygolfclubs.com*

OPENING HOURS:
Monday to Saturday
6:30am – 12am

GOOD FOR HOSTING...
...an afternoon of bonding and interacting with a group of 4 or more colleagues and clients.
...a launch party for up to 250 guests that could integrate the use of the simulators and consoles.

LOCATION: The City
NEAREST TUBE: Bank
FUNCTION ROOMS: 1
CAPACITY: 250 standing
PRIVATE DINING: N/A
CIVIL CEREMONIES: No
CUISINE: Flexible catering

CLARIDGE'S
A HOTEL

"A name synonymous with style, glamour and exceptional service; Claridge's remains at the forefront of London's hotel scene."

Brook Street, London W1K 4HR
T: *020 7629 8860* W: *www.claridges.co.uk*

GOOD FOR GOING OUT...

...for after-work drinks with a client in **Claridge's Bar**.

...for afternoon tea in **The Foyer** with someone sophisticated you want to impress.

...for a celebratory dinner in **Gordon Ramsay at Claridge's**.

GOOD FOR HOSTING...

...a cocktail party in **The Fumoir** to network with colleagues and clients.

...a prestigious lunch meeting in an intimately stylish private dining room.

...a grand wedding in the spectacular **Ballroom**.

...an impressive and glamorous party in the **Art Deco Ballroom Reception**.

LOCATION: Mayfair
NEAREST TUBE: Bond Street
FUNCTION ROOMS: 10
CAPACITY: 240 seated / 450 standing
PRIVATE DINING: 6, 20, 50, 96, 120, 240
CIVIL CEREMONIES: Yes
CUISINE: British / Afternoon Tea

REVIEW ONLINE

THE CONNAUGHT
A HOTEL

"With a luxury spa, two legendary bars and one of London's top chefs on site, The Connaught is a stalwart luxury hotel in Mayfair."

Carlos Place, London W1K 2AL
T: *020 7499 7070* W: *www.the-connaught.co.uk*

GOOD FOR GOING OUT...

...for exceptional pre-dinner cocktails in the elegant and luxurious **Connaught Bar**, when no expense is spared.

...for a traditional tea in a light, airy and very refined setting.

...for a fabulous dinner in **Hélène Darroze's** restaurant to celebrate a special occasion with your husband or wife.

GOOD FOR HOSTING...

...a stylish cocktail party for discerning guests in **The Ballroom**.

...a sophisticated launch party in **The Maple Room**.

...an intimate dinner for up to 8 people at **The Sommelier's Table**.

LOCATION: Mayfair
NEAREST TUBE: Bond Street
FUNCTION ROOMS: 7
CAPACITY: 120 seated / 200 standing
PRIVATE DINING: 12, 20, 60, 120
CIVIL CEREMONIES: Yes
CUISINE: French / Afternoon Tea

CORRIGAN'S
A RESTAURANT

"Simultaneously sophisticated and homely, with Corrigan's, Richard Corrigan has added another exceptional restaurant to his portfolio."

28 Upper Grosvenor Street, London W1K 7EH
T: *020 7499 9943* W: *www.corrigansmayfair.com*

OPENING HOURS:
Monday to Friday / Saturday / Sunday
12pm – 3pm / Closed / 12pm – 4pm;
6pm – 11pm / 6pm – 11pm / 6pm – 9:30pm

GOOD FOR GOING OUT...
...for a special occasion with your family, to enjoy hearty British cuisine in a stylish setting.
...for dinner with clients who value good food and wine.
...for a dinner date where you want to be able to talk and relax.

GOOD FOR HOSTING...
...a business lunch for up to 30 important clients.
...a unique dining experience for up to 12 people at the traditional and stylish **Chef's Table**, which can have a full view of the kitchen or be closed off for complete privacy.

LOCATION: Mayfair
NEAREST TUBE: Marble Arch
FUNCTION ROOMS: 4
CAPACITY: 70 seated
PRIVATE DINING: 6, 12, 30, 70
CIVIL CEREMONIES: No
CUISINE: British

CRAZY BEAR
A PRIVATE MEMBERS' CLUB

"This fourth Crazy Bear site in Covent Garden is for members only but offers a bold, fun and sexy setting for private events."

17 Mercer Street, London WC2H 9QJ
T: *020 7520 5450* W: *www.crazybeargroup.co.uk/coventgarden*

OPENING HOURS:
Monday to Saturday
10am – 1am

GOOD FOR GOING OUT...
...if you're lucky enough to be a member.

GOOD FOR HOSTING...
...a birthday party with a decadent and hedonistic vibe in the lounge bar.
...an informal but vibrant private dinner with clients in the private dining room for up to 40 people.
...an opulent and flamboyant cocktail and canapé party for 135 people.

LOCATION: West End
NEAREST TUBE: Covent Garden
FUNCTION ROOMS: 4
CAPACITY: 40 seated / 135 standing
PRIVATE DINING: 40
CIVIL CEREMONIES: No
CUISINE: Pan Asian

THE CUCKOO CLUB
A RESTAURANT, BAR & NIGHTCLUB

"A 'rock 'n' regal' interior draws out the party gene in even the most retiring visitor."

Swallow Street, London W1B 4EZ
T: *020 7287 4300* W: *www.thecuckooclub.com*

OPENING HOURS:
Wednesday to Saturday
8pm – late

GOOD FOR GOING OUT...
...for a fun-fueled dinner in the restaurant with a group of
   friends, before dancing the night away in an opulent setting.
...for a night of dancing with a jetset crowd.

GOOD FOR HOSTING...
...a private and lavish dinner in the decadent and atmospheric
   restaurant, with a private cocktail bar and dancing.
...a no-holds-barred corporate event that combines sex appeal
   with sophistication in a complete venue takeover.

LOCATION: Mayfair
NEAREST TUBE: Piccadilly Circus
FUNCTION ROOMS: 2
CAPACITY: 80 seated / 300 standing
PRIVATE DINING: 80
CIVIL CEREMONIES: No
CUISINE: Modern European

DAPHNE'S
A RESTAURANT

"Full of charm all year round, this understated but chic Italian restaurant is a gem in the South Ken area."

112 Draycott Avenue, London SW3 3AE
T: *020 7387 5277* W: *www.daphnes-restaurant.co.uk*

OPENING HOURS:
Monday to Friday / Saturday / Sunday
12pm – 3pm; 5:30pm – 11:30pm / 12pm – 11:30pm /
12pm – 10:30pm

GOOD FOR GOING OUT...
...for lunch in elegant surroundings with your mother.
...for a relaxed dinner with friends in a chic and
   welcoming setting.
...for a low-key, romantic dinner with your partner.

GOOD FOR HOSTING...
...an alfresco birthday lunch or dinner in the **Conservatory**
   for up to 40 people in the Summer months.
...a dinner party for up to 40 people in the charming
   Conservatory in front of the open log fire.

LOCATION: South Kensington
NEAREST TUBE: South Kensington
FUNCTION ROOMS: 1
CAPACITY: 40 seated / 50 standing
PRIVATE DINING: 40
CIVIL CEREMONIES: No
CUISINE: Italian

DEAN STREET TOWNHOUSE
A RESTAURANT

"This Georgian townhouse is a relaxed and stylish setting in the heart of Soho, suited to almost all occasions, at all times of day."

69-71 Dean Street, London W1D 3SE
T: *020 7434 1775* W: *www.deanstreettownhouse.com*

OPENING HOURS:
Monday to Thursday / Friday / Saturday
7am – 12am / 7am – 1am / 8am – 1am

GOOD FOR GOING OUT...
...for an informal meeting with a client.
...for a catch up with a friend over a glass of wine and bite
   to eat, sitting at the bar.
...for afternoon tea with colleagues for a brainstorm.
...for a first date in a relaxed but sparkling atmosphere.
...for dinner with a partner before an overnight stay in
   a stylish bedroom upstairs.

GOOD FOR HOSTING...
...a business meeting for up to 12 fun-loving clients in the
   charming private dining room.

LOCATION: Soho
NEAREST TUBE: Leicester Square
FUNCTION ROOMS: 1
CAPACITY: 12 seated / 20 standing
PRIVATE DINING: 12
CIVIL CEREMONIES: No
CUISINE: Modern European

THE DECK
AN EVENT SPACE

"The Deck is a unique and stylish roof-top event space at the National Theatre, with translucent walls allowing for views across the river and city beyond."

National Theatre, South Bank, London SE1 9PX
T: *020 7452 3931 / 3796*
W: *www.nationaltheatre.org.uk/thedeck*

OPENING HOURS:
Open daily for events and private hire

GOOD FOR HOSTING...
...a product launch in a blank canvas space during the
   day for up to 120 guests.
...an alfresco barbecue with cocktails and spectacular
   nighttime views of London's skyline.
...a unique wedding or civil partnership with a sit down
   dinner to a backdrop of London's twinkling lights.

LOCATION: South Bank
NEAREST TUBE: Waterloo
FUNCTION ROOMS: 1
CAPACITY: 80 seated / 120 standing
PRIVATE DINING: 80
CIVIL CEREMONIES: Yes
CUISINE: Flexible catering

DINNER
BY HESTON BLUMENTHAL
A RESTAURANT

"A runaway hit even before it opened, Heston Blumenthal's first London venture is widely regarded as 'blumen' marvellous."

Mandarin Oriental, 66 Knightsbridge, London SW1X 7LA
T: *020 7235 2000* W: *www.dinnerbyheston.com*

OPENING HOURS:
Open daily
12pm – 2:30pm; 6:30pm – 10:30pm

GOOD FOR GOING OUT...
...with someone who has booked a table well in advance.
...to sample inventive and masterful gastronomy in a
    unique setting overlooking the park.
...for a relaxed lunch with clients to entertain and impress.
...for a special dinner with your husband or wife.

GOOD FOR HOSTING...
...an intimate and relaxed dinner for a unique experience
    in the private dining room with up to 10 guests.

LOCATION: Knightsbridge
NEAREST TUBE: Knightsbridge
FUNCTION ROOMS: 1
CAPACITY: 10 seated
PRIVATE DINING: 10
CIVIL CEREMONIES: No
CUISINE: British

DISHOOM
A RESTAURANT

"A Bombay-style café, bustling and atmospheric, Dishoom is a top destination all through the day."

12 Upper St Martins Lane, London WC2H 9FB
T: *020 7420 9320* W: *www.dishoom.com*
OPENING HOURS:
Monday to Friday / Saturday / Sunday
8am – 11pm / 10am – 11pm / 10am – 10pm

GOOD FOR GOING OUT...
...for a delicious breakfast with a difference, with your
    boyfriend or girlfriend.
...for a relaxed lunch or cup of chai tea to catch up with
    a friend.
...with a group of friends to sample some simple but
    delicious Indian cuisine.

GOOD FOR HOSTING...
...a dinner in the atmospheric and stylish basement restaurant.
...a Christmas drinks reception for up to 80 guests in this
    wonderfully Central location.

LOCATION: West End
NEAREST TUBE: Leicester Square
FUNCTION ROOMS: 1
CAPACITY: 80 seated / 80 standing
PRIVATE DINING: 80
CIVIL CEREMONIES: No
CUISINE: Indian

THE DORCHESTER
A HOTEL

"Home to Alain Ducasse, China Tang, The Krug Room and other impeccable spaces for going out and holding events, The Dorchester has it all."

Park Lane, London W1K 1QA
T: *020 7629 8888* W: *www.thedorchester.com*

GOOD FOR GOING OUT...

...for an anniversary dinner at **Alain Ducasse** with a discerning connoisseur of French cuisine.
...for an impressive client lunch that showcases the finest in Cantonese cuisine at **China Tang**.
...for a traditional afternoon tea in **The Promenade** to celebrate a birthday with girlfriends.

GOOD FOR HOSTING...

...a wedding banquet with wow factor in **The Ballroom**.
...a cocktail party for a product launch in the **Orchid Room**.
...an intimate and unique dinner in **The Krug Room** with a mixed group of up to 12 guests.
...a special occasion with your girlfriends in **The Spatisserie**.

The Krug Room at The Dorchester

LOCATION: Mayfair
NEAREST TUBE: Hyde Park Corner
FUNCTION ROOMS: 11
CAPACITY: 500 seated / 1,000 standing
PRIVATE DINING: 12, 34, 60, 140, 500
CIVIL CEREMONIES: Yes
CUISINE: French / Cantonese / Tea

DUKES HOTEL
A HOTEL

"Discreetly nestled in Mayfair, this five star hotel oozes with traditional British charm."

St. James's Place, London SW1A 1NY
T: *020 7491 4840* W: *www.dukeshotel.com*

GOOD FOR GOING OUT...

...on a date to sample the infamously lethal but delicious martini cocktail served in **Dukes Bar**.

GOOD FOR HOSTING...

...a traditional wedding in a comfortable and luxurious setting with a thoughtful and energetic in-house team.
...an intimate candlelit dinner in **The Sheridan Room** for 12 guests.
...a chic and elegant drinks party for up to 120 discerning guests in **The Marlborough Suite**.

LOCATION: Mayfair
NEAREST TUBE: Green Park
FUNCTION ROOMS: 4
CAPACITY: 60 seated / 120 standing
PRIVATE DINING: 12, 14, 60
CIVIL CEREMONIES: Yes
CUISINE: British

E&O
A RESTAURANT

"E&O is chic and sleek. With a vibrant bar and upbeat restaurant, it is a favourite with well-heeled and fun-loving locals."

14 Blenheim Crescent, London W11 1NN
T: *020 7229 5454* W: *www.rickerrestaurants.com/eando*

OPENING HOURS:
Monday to Saturday
12pm – 12am
Sunday
12:30pm – 11:30pm

GOOD FOR GOING OUT...
...for after-work cocktails with a fashionista friend.
...on a first date, for cocktails followed by dinner in elegant and buzzy surroundings.
...for a fun catch up with a group of friends.

LOCATION: Notting Hill
NEAREST TUBE: Ladbroke Grove
FUNCTION ROOMS: 1
CAPACITY: 18 seated
PRIVATE DINING: 18
CIVIL CEREMONIES: No
CUISINE: Pan Asian

EDF ENERGY LONDON EYE
AN EVENT SPACE

"An iconic venue, The London Eye offers a memorable experience for corporate events."

County Hall, Westminster Bridge Road, London SE1 7PB
T: *0871 222 4002* W: *www.londoneye.com*

OPENING HOURS:
Open daily for events and private hire

GOOD FOR HOSTING...
...a drinks party for up to 25 guests in a private capsule.
...a ***Champagne experience*** to entertain and impress clients from out of town.

LOCATION: Southbank
NEAREST TUBE: Waterloo
FUNCTION ROOMS: 32
CAPACITY: 25 standing
PRIVATE DINING: N/A
CIVIL CEREMONIES: Yes
CUISINE: Flexible catering

EMBASSY LONDON
A RESTAURANT, BAR & NIGHTCLUB

"Embassy offers a bar, restaurant and club in the heart of Mayfair meaning a whole night can unfold under one roof."

29 Old Burlington Street, London W1S 3AN
T: *020 7851 0956* W: *www.embassylondon.com*

OPENING HOURS:
Wednesday to Saturday
Restaurant: 6pm – 11pm (bar snacks until 1am)
Members' Club: 10pm – 3am

GOOD FOR GOING OUT...
...on a night out with clients, for cocktails followed by
  dinner and then drinks and dancing in the club.
...to enjoy modern European cuisine on the small heated
  terrace with friends, on a Summer evening.
...dancing with friends in the sleek, stylish club.

GOOD FOR HOSTING...
...an early evening drinks party in the restaurant and bar,
  with the opportunity to exhibit art work.
...a glamorous gala evening by taking over the whole venue.

LOCATION: Mayfair
NEAREST TUBE: Green Park
FUNCTION ROOMS: 4
CAPACITY: 450 standing
PRIVATE DINING: N/A
CIVIL CEREMONIES: No
CUISINE: Modern European

FRANCO'S
A RESTAURANT

"From breakfast through to dinner via lunches and early evening drinks, Franco's is a favourite with Mayfair locals and others who want an eyeful of a certain rather risqué painting..."

61 Jermyn Street, London SW1Y 6LX
T: *020 7499 2211* W: *www.francoslondon.com*

OPENING HOURS:
Monday to Friday / Saturday
7:30am – 11pm / 8am – 11:30pm

GOOD FOR GOING OUT...
...for an informal business breakfast.
...for a relaxed, low-key, great value but sophisticated
  lunch with a client.
...for a catch up with your family, over dinner.
...for an alfresco, after-work glass of rosé.

GOOD FOR HOSTING...
...an intimate and relaxed dinner with colleagues in
  the private dining room for up to 50 guests.
...a fun Christmas party followed by music and dancing.

LOCATION: Mayfair
NEAREST TUBE: Green Park
FUNCTION ROOMS: 3
CAPACITY: 70 seated / 120 standing
PRIVATE DINING: 18, 30, 70
CIVIL CEREMONIES: No
CUISINE: Italian

GALVIN AT WINDOWS
A RESTAURANT

"For views, Michelin-starred French cuisine, a sophisticated setting and impeccable service, this fantastic restaurant by the unstoppable Galvin brothers is hard to beat."

London Hilton, 22 Park Lane, London W1K 1BE
T: *020 7208 4021* W: *www.galvinatwindows.com*

OPENING HOURS:
Monday to Wednesday / Thursday and Friday
12pm – 2:30pm; 6pm – 10:30pm / 12pm – 2:30pm; 6pm – 11pm
Saturday / Sunday
6pm – 11pm / 11:45am – 3pm

GOOD FOR GOING OUT...
...to admire the view over cocktails in the sophisticated bar.
...for a formal lunch where seamless service is a must.
...for an anniversary dinner and drinks with your spouse.

GOOD FOR HOSTING...
...an exceptional and memorable private dinner for up to 30 guests, in the semi-private dining space that offers miraculous London views.

LOCATION: Mayfair
NEAREST TUBE: Hyde Park Corner
FUNCTION ROOMS: 2
CAPACITY: 120 seated / 150 standing
PRIVATE DINING: 30, 120
CIVIL CEREMONIES: Yes
CUISINE: French

GRAY'S INN
AN EVENT SPACE

"One of the four Ancient Inns of Court, Gray's Inn offers an exclusive oasis of tradition and calm."

8 South Square, London WC1R 5ET
T: *020 7458 7830* W: *www.graysinnbanqueting.com*

OPENING HOURS:
Open daily for events and private hire

GOOD FOR HOSTING...
...a candlelit banquet in ***The Hall*** with wood paneling adding grandeur and an inimitable atmosphere.
...a formal and traditional lunch meeting for clients.

LOCATION: The City
NEAREST TUBE: Chancery Lane
FUNCTION ROOMS: 6
CAPACITY: 188 seated / 350 standing
PRIVATE DINING: 12, 16, 70, 80, 188
CIVIL CEREMONIES: Yes
CUISINE: Flexible catering

THE GRAZING GOAT

A PUBLIC HOUSE & HOTEL

"From the team behind the ever-buzzing Orange, Pantechnicon and Thomas Cubitt, The Grazing Goat isn't for billy-no-mates."

6 New Quebec Street, London W1H 7RQ
T: *020 7724 7243* W: *www.thegrazinggoat.co.uk*

OPENING HOURS:
Monday to Saturday / Sunday
7:30am – 11:30pm / 7:30am – 10:30pm

GOOD FOR GOING OUT...
...for an informal business breakfast.
...for a relaxed lunch away from the hordes of Oxford Street.
...for after-work drinks in a countryside pub atmosphere.
...for a low-key but fun dinner with friends.

GOOD FOR HOSTING...
...an informal but refined birthday drinks party and dinner for close friends and family.
...a relaxed Christmas dinner party with colleagues in a rustic and chic setting.

LOCATION: Marble Arch / Marylebone
NEAREST TUBE: Marble Arch
FUNCTION ROOMS: 2
CAPACITY: 60 seated / 100 standing
PRIVATE DINING: 32, 60
CIVIL CEREMONIES: No
CUISINE: British

HAKKASAN MAYFAIR

A RESTAURANT

"Hakkasan Mayfair – the second Hakkasan to open in London – offers a buzzy and sophisticated destination for cocktails and exquisite Chinese cuisine."

17 Bruton Street, London W1J 6QB
T: *020 7907 1888* W: *w3.hakkasan.com / mayfair*

OPENING HOURS:
Monday to Friday / Saturday and Sunday
Restaurant: 12pm – 3:15pm / 12pm – 4:15pm; 6pm – 10pm
Bar: 12pm – 11:30pm

GOOD FOR GOING OUT...
...for pre-dinner drinks in the glamorous bar with someone flash.
...for lunch to enjoy a good value dim sum feast.
...for an indulgent dinner to celebrate a special occasion with friends.

GOOD FOR HOSTING...
...a decadent dinner in the private dining room to impress clients.

LOCATION: Mayfair
NEAREST TUBE: Green Park
FUNCTION ROOMS: 2
CAPACITY: 220 seated / 275 standing
PRIVATE DINING: 14, 220
CIVIL CEREMONIES: No
CUISINE: Chinese

HAWKSMOOR
A RESTAURANT

"Fantastic steak, a fun crowd, fabulous service and a relaxed vibe – what more do you want?"

157 Commercial Street, London E1 6BJ
T: 020 7247 7392 W: www.thehawksmoor.com

OPENING HOURS:
Monday to Friday
12pm – 3pm; 6pm – 12am
Saturday and Sunday
11am – 4pm; 6pm – 12am (closed Sunday dinner)

GOOD FOR GOING OUT...
...for an informal but sophisticated client lunch.
...for a birthday dinner with a group of friends.

GOOD FOR HOSTING...
...a lunch party for up to 14 people in a private area, or up to 10 in the restaurant itself.

LOCATION: Shoreditch
NEAREST TUBE: Shoreditch High St
FUNCTION ROOMS: 1
CAPACITY: 14 seated
PRIVATE DINING: 14
CIVIL CEREMONIES: No
CUISINE: Steak

HIBISCUS
A RESTAURANT

"Hibiscus offers Michelin-starred food and service in an ambiance well-suited to special occasions."

29 Maddox Street, London W1S 2PA
T: 020 7629 2999 W: www.hibiscusrestaurant.co.uk

OPENING HOURS:
Monday to Thursday
12pm – 3pm; 6pm – 11pm
Friday and Saturday
12pm – 4pm; 6pm – 11:30pm

GOOD FOR GOING OUT...
...for dinner with a connoisseur of French cuisine.
...for an anniversary dinner with your husband or wife in a romantic and refined setting.
...for an indulgent and formal client lunch.

GOOD FOR HOSTING...
...a discreet but exceptional feast for up to 18 people in the elegant private dining room.

LOCATION: Mayfair
NEAREST TUBE: Oxford Circus
FUNCTION ROOMS: 2
CAPACITY: 45 seated
PRIVATE DINING: 18, 45
CIVIL CEREMONIES: No
CUISINE: French

HIX SOHO
A RESTAURANT & BAR

"Is it worthy of the hype? I'd say so; a night here tends to go without a 'hix'."

70 Brewer St, London W1F 9TR
T: *020 7292 3518* W: *www.hixsoho.co.uk*

OPENING HOURS:
Monday to Saturday / Sunday
12pm – 11:30pm / 12pm – 10:30pm

GOOD FOR GOING OUT...
...for pre- and post-theatre dining with a date.
...on a date to enjoy the buzzing atmosphere in theatreland, the seasonal British menu and **Mark's Bar** for post dinner drinks.
...a fun and vibrant dinner with clients.

GOOD FOR HOSTING...
...a Christmas drinks party for up to 80 people in **Mark's Bar** with colleagues and clients.
...a working lunch in the private dining room for up to 10 people.

LOCATION: Soho
NEAREST TUBE: Piccadilly Circus
FUNCTION ROOMS: 3
CAPACITY: 80 seated / 220 standing
PRIVATE DINING: 10, 36, 80
CIVIL CEREMONIES: No
CUISINE: British

HOME HOUSE
A PRIVATE MEMBERS' CLUB

"This private members' club sees a marriage of the traditional and the modern in an impressive and versatile setting off Portman Square."

REVIEW ONLINE

20 Portman Square, London W1H 6LW
T: *020 7670 2000* W: *www.homehouse.co.uk*

OPENING HOURS:
Open daily
7am – 1am

GOOD FOR GOING OUT...
...if you're lucky enough to be a member.

GOOD FOR HOSTING...
...a lavish wedding in the spectacular garden.
...a launch party with live entertainment.
...an intimate private lunch in **The Front Parlour**.
...a candlelit cocktail party for up to 40 guests in **The Asylum Room**.
...a Summer drinks party in **Portman Square Gardens**.

LOCATION: Marylebone
NEAREST TUBE: Marble Arch
FUNCTION ROOMS: 5
CAPACITY: 80 seated / 200 standing
PRIVATE DINING: 22, 80
CIVIL CEREMONIES: Yes
CUISINE: Modern European

THE HOSPITAL CLUB
A PRIVATE MEMBERS' CLUB

"If you eat, drink and sleep media, then you should eat, drink and sleep at The Hospital Club."

24 Endell Street, London WC2H 9HQ
T: *020 7170 9100* W: *www.thehospitalclub.com*

OPENING HOURS:
Monday to Friday / Saturday
8am / 11am – 2am

GOOD FOR GOING OUT...
...if you're lucky enough to be a member.

GOOD FOR HOSTING...
...a launch party or exhibition in the blank canvas *Gallery*.
...a screening complete with 3D capabilities.
...a relaxed drinks party for up to 30 guests in the *Bellini Bar*.
...a light and airy meeting in *The Library* to get creative juices flowing.
...a bonding session with colleagues and clients in *The Games Room*.
...a sit down dinner in the *First Floor* or the *Forest Room*.

LOCATION: West End
NEAREST TUBE: Covent Garden
FUNCTION ROOMS: 10
CAPACITY: 150 seated / 300 standing
PRIVATE DINING: 8, 12, 18, 30, 35, 150
CIVIL CEREMONIES: Yes
CUISINE: British

THE HURLINGHAM CLUB
A PRIVATE MEMBERS' CLUB

"An idyllic oasis, this members' club housed in a Georgian country house surrounded by landscaped gardens is one of London's most precious spots."

Ranelagh Gardens, London SW6 3PR
T: *020 7471 8220* W: *www.hurlinghamclub.org.uk*

OPENING HOURS:
Open daily
12pm – 3pm; 6pm – 11pm

GOOD FOR GOING OUT...
...if you're lucky enough to be a member.

GOOD FOR HOSTING...
...a breathtaking wedding in a picturesque setting.
...a dinner-dance for a discerning crowd following early evening alfresco reception drinks during the Summer.

LOCATION: Fulham
NEAREST TUBE: Putney Bridge
FUNCTION ROOMS: 7
CAPACITY: 1,000 seated / 1,200 standing
PRIVATE DINING: 14, 60, 95, 350, 1,000
CIVIL CEREMONIES: Yes
CUISINE: British

INDIGO2
AN EVENT SPACE

"The O2 is one of the most iconic spaces in London but the main arena is not the only space available for private hire."

Peninsula Square, London SE10 0DX
T: *020 8463 2000* W: *www.theo2.co.uk/indigo2*

OPENING HOURS:
Open daily for events and private hire

GOOD FOR HOSTING...
...a corporate event with live performances for up to 1,623 people (to be precise).
...an awards ceremony with lavish and impressive décor.
...a fashion show followed by a club night for a trendy crowd.
...a large scale extravaganza with state-of-the-art lighting, effects and AV.
...VIP hospitality surrounding an O2 Arena show.

LOCATION: Greenwich
NEAREST TUBE: North Greenwich
FUNCTION ROOMS: 3
CAPACITY: 1,623 seated
PRIVATE DINING: N/A
CIVIL CEREMONIES: No
CUISINE: Flexible catering

INNER TEMPLE
AN EVENT SPACE

"This Ancient Inn of Court is a world unto its own; a charming place for any event."

Inner Temple, London EC4Y 7HL
T: *020 7797 8230* W: *www.innertemplecatering.org.uk*

OPENING HOURS:
Open daily for events and private hire

GOOD FOR HOSTING...
...a large client reception in traditional, historical surroundings.
...a sumptuous wedding banquet with both indoor and outdoor space.

LOCATION: Embankment
NEAREST TUBE: Temple
FUNCTION ROOMS: 5
CAPACITY: 200 seated / 400 standing
PRIVATE DINING: 12, 30, 50, 90, 200
CIVIL CEREMONIES: Yes
CUISINE: Flexible catering

THE IVY
A RESTAURANT

"For many The Ivy is more than just a restaurant; it is an institution."

1-5 West Street, London WC2H 9NQ
T: *020 7836 4751* W: *www.the-ivy.co.uk*

OPENING HOURS:
Monday to Saturday / Sunday
12pm – 3pm / 12pm – 3:30pm; 5:30pm – 12am / 5:30pm – 11pm

GOOD FOR GOING OUT…
…for a pre-theatre dinner with your parents, and post-theatre dinner with a date.
…for a buzzy lunch with clients.
…for a special occasion with a small group of friends.

GOOD FOR HOSTING…
…a drinks and canapé reception for up to 120 clients, to the sound of a baby grand.
…a candlelit, atmospheric dinner party to celebrate with up to 60 friends.
…a lunch meeting for up to 32 people at one table, or 60 on 6 round tables.

LOCATION: Covent Garden
NEAREST TUBE: Leicester Square
FUNCTION ROOMS: 1
CAPACITY: 60 seated / 120 standing
PRIVATE DINING: 60
CIVIL CEREMONIES: No
CUISINE: British / International

J SHEEKEY
& J SHEEKEY OYSTER BAR
A RESTAURANT & BAR

"A theatreland classic with a fish pie as famous as many of its visitors."

28-32 St Martin's Court, London WC2N 4AL
T: *020 7240 2565* W: *www.j-sheekey.co.uk*

OPENING HOURS:
Monday to Saturday
Restaurant: 12pm – 3pm; 5:30pm – 12am
Oyster Bar: 12pm – 12am
Sunday
Restaurant: 12pm – 3pm; 6pm – 11pm
Oyster Bar: 12pm – 11pm

GOOD FOR GOING OUT…
…for pre-and post-theatre dining in a charming and welcoming setting.
…for a relaxed but chic date in the **Oyster Bar** with a lover of seafood.

LOCATION: Covent Garden
NEAREST TUBE: Leicester Square
FUNCTION ROOMS: 0
CAPACITY: 6 seated
PRIVATE DINING: N/A
CIVIL CEREMONIES: No
CUISINE: British / Seafood / Oysters

THE KING PIN SUITE AT BLOOMSBURY LANES
A BOWLING ALLEY

"Bloomsbury Lanes is for exhibitionists who want to bowl, sing, drink and dance."

Tavistock Hotel, Bedford Way, London WC1H 9EU
T: *020 7183 1979* W: *www.bloomsburybowling.com*

OPENING HOURS:
Sunday to Thursday / Friday and Saturday
1pm – 12am / 3am

GOOD FOR GOING OUT...
...after work with friends to drink, bowl and unwind.
...with a date to do something fun and different in a charming and stylish setting.

GOOD FOR HOSTING...
...a karaoke party for 6 – 30 people in relaxed and vibrant surroundings.
...an entertainment-fueled party with cocktails, bowling, karaoke and dancing options in the decadent **King Pin Suite**, for up to 250 people.

LOCATION: Bloomsbury
NEAREST TUBE: Russell Square
FUNCTION ROOMS: 2
CAPACITY: 250 standing
PRIVATE DINING: N/A
CIVIL CEREMONIES: No
CUISINE: American

KOPAPA
A RESTAURANT

"From the same team that set up the highly acclaimed Providores, Kopapa is another all-day-dining hit."

32 – 34 Monmouth Street, London WC2H 9HA
T: *020 7240 6076* W: *www.kopapa.co.uk*

OPENING HOURS:
Monday to Thursday / Friday
8:30am – 10:45pm / 8:30am – 11:15pm
Saturday / Sunday
10am – 11:15pm / 10am – 9:45pm

GOOD FOR GOING OUT...
...for a relaxed and hearty breakfast with your girlfriend or boyfriend.
...for an informal lunch with your friends.
...for a low-key dinner to unwind and enjoy creative fusion food.

LOCATION: West End
NEAREST TUBE: Covent Garden
FUNCTION ROOMS: 1
CAPACITY: 60 seated / 80 standing
PRIVATE DINING: 60
CIVIL CEREMONIES: No
CUISINE: Modern European / Fusion

LOCATION: Chelsea
NEAREST TUBE: Gloucester Road
FUNCTION ROOMS: 2
CAPACITY: 120 standing
PRIVATE DINING: N/A
CIVIL CEREMONIES: No
CUISINE: Bar snacks / Canapés

KOSMOPOL
A BAR & NIGHTCLUB

"Kosmopol is like many men's dream girl; petite, perfectly formed and Swedish, with both a quiet, intimate side and a carefree, naughty side."

138 Fulham Road, London SW10 9PY
T: *020 7373 6368* W: *www.kosmopollondon.co.uk*

OPENING HOURS:
Monday to Thursday / Friday and Saturday / Sunday
5pm – 1am / 5pm – 2am / 5pm – 12:30am

GOOD FOR GOING OUT...
...for relaxed midweek drinks and a catch up with a friend.
...on a Friday or Saturday night for a night of delicious cocktails and dancing until the early hours.

GOOD FOR HOSTING...
...a birthday party with cocktails and dancing to a DJ on the decks with up to 80 friends, in a relaxed and effortlessly cool setting.

LOCATION: Marylebone
NEAREST TUBE: Marylebone
FUNCTION ROOMS: 11
CAPACITY: 504 seated / 750 standing
PRIVATE DINING: N/A
CIVIL CEREMONIES: Yes
CUISINE: British / Afternoon Tea

THE LANDMARK
A HOTEL

"Whether for business or pleasure, this five star hotel caters to your every need, making it a landmark by name and by nature."

222 Marylebone Road, London NW1 6JQ
T: *020 7631 8000* W: *www.landmarklondon.co.uk*

GOOD FOR GOING OUT...
...for a low-key breakfast meeting.
...for a low-key lunch with clients in the welcoming setting of ***twotwentytwo Restaurant and Bar***.

GOOD FOR HOSTING...
...a lavish banquet in ***The Grand Ballroom*** after a dramatic entrance through the atrium of the hotel.
...glamorous Champagne receptions in traditional surroundings.

LE CAPRICE
A RESTAURANT

"A reliable, timeless classic, Le Caprice fits the bill for almost any occasion."

Arlington Street, London SW1A 1RJ
T: *020 7629 2239* W: *www.le-caprice.co.uk*

OPENING HOURS:
Monday to Thursday / Friday and Saturday
12pm – 3pm / 4pm; 5.30pm – 12am
Sunday
11:30am – 11pm

GOOD FOR GOING OUT...
...for a refined business lunch.
...to meet the in-laws in an elegant setting.
...to catch up with glamorous girlfriends.
...for a pre-theatre dinner to impress a date.

GOOD FOR HOSTING...
...groups of up to 8 in the semi-private dining room.

LOCATION: St James
NEAREST TUBE: Green Park
FUNCTION ROOMS: 0
CAPACITY: 8 seated
PRIVATE DINING: N/A
CIVIL CEREMONIES: No
CUISINE: Modern European

THE LEDBURY
A RESTAURANT

"The Ledbury offers two-Michelin-starred food in the heart of Notting Hill in a formal setting."

127 Ledbury Road, London W11 2AQ
T: *020 7792 9090* W: *www.theledbury.com*

OPENING HOURS:
Monday to Saturday
12pm – 2:30pm (closed Monday lunch); 6:30pm – 10:30pm
Sunday
12pm – 3pm; 7pm – 10pm

GOOD FOR GOING OUT...
...for a sophisticated lunch to celebrate a special occasion with friends and family.
...for a birthday dinner with your husband or wife.
...for exquisite alfresco dining.

GOOD FOR HOSTING...
...a celebration with an indulgent take over of the whole restaurant.

LOCATION: Notting Hill
NEAREST TUBE: Westbourne Park
FUNCTION ROOMS: N/A
CAPACITY: N/A
PRIVATE DINING: N/A
CIVIL CEREMONIES: No
CUISINE: British

LES DEUX SALONS
A RESTAURANT

"This traditional French brasserie is the third offering from the team behind Wild Honey and Arbutus."

40-42 William IV Street, London WC2N 4DD
T: *020 7420 2050* W: *www.lesdeuxsalons.co.uk*

OPENING HOURS:
Open daily
12pm – 11pm

GOOD FOR GOING OUT...
...for a relaxed but refined working lunch with clients.
...for a date with someone chic and sociable.

GOOD FOR HOSTING...
...a relaxed lunch with up to 10 clients in the privacy of a
  private dining room.
...a low-key private dinner with a group of up to 25 friends,
  with your own music.

LOCATION: West End
NEAREST TUBE: Charing Cross
FUNCTION ROOMS: 3
CAPACITY: 150 seated / 300 standing
PRIVATE DINING: 10, 25, 150
CIVIL CEREMONIES: No
CUISINE: French

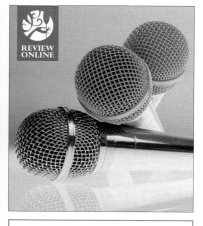

REVIEW
ONLINE

LUCKY VOICE
A KARAOKE BAR

"If it's a party of uninhibited fun or a midweek pick-me-up with friends you need, head to Lucky Voice without delay."

52 Poland Street London W1F 7NQ
T: *020 7439 3660* W: *www.luckyvoice.com*

OPENING HOURS:
Monday to Thursday / Friday and Saturday / Sunday
5:30pm – 1am / 3pm – 1am / 3pm – 10:30pm

GOOD FOR GOING OUT...
...with a group of friends for some no-holds-barred fun.
...to serenade a loved one.
...for a fun and bonding night with carefree colleagues.

GOOD FOR HOSTING...
...a birthday party with an all-inclusive package.
...a hen party with a difference because *Girls Just Wanna
  Have Fun.*
...a karaoke party in your home with their **Lucky Voice
  Party Box**.

LOCATION: Soho
NEAREST TUBE: Oxford Circus
FUNCTION ROOMS: 10
CAPACITY: 130 standing
PRIVATE DINING: N/A
CIVIL CEREMONIES: No
CUISINE: Pizza / Bar snacks

LUTYENS
A RESTAURANT

"A sophisticated, stylish offering from Conran and Prescott with a discreet private members' club to suit all your business needs."

85 Fleet Street, London EC4Y 1AE
T: *020 7583 8385* W: *www.lutyens-restaurant.com*

OPENING HOURS:
Monday to Friday
7:30am – 12am

GOOD FOR GOING OUT...
...for a formal lunch with clients.
...to have a sophisticated dinner of delicious French
   cuisine and exceptional wines.
...for an informal and low-key breakfast in the bar.

GOOD FOR HOSTING...
...a sophisticated working lunch in a private dining
   room, with discerning clients.
... a formal or informal event with exclusive hire of
   the entire venue.

LOCATION: The City
NEAREST TUBE: Blackfriars
FUNCTION ROOMS: 4
CAPACITY: 120 seated / 250 standing
PRIVATE DINING: 6, 12, 16, 26, 120
CIVIL CEREMONIES: No
CUISINE: French / Seafood

MADAME TUSSAUDS
AN EVENT SPACE

"Host an event at this world-renowned, big capacity venue, and your guests will be waxing lyrical forevermore."

Marylebone Road, London NW1 5LR
T: *0844 824 6269* W: *www.merlineventslondon.com*

OPENING HOURS:
Open daily for events and private hire

GOOD FOR HOSTING...
...a lavish awards dinner in the **World Stage Ballroom** with
   live entertainment and opulent decor to add wow factor.
...a private, after-hours VIP tour before a sit-down dinner
   to entertain clients.
...a fun and interactive children's party.

LOCATION: Marylebone
NEAREST TUBE: Baker Street
FUNCTION ROOMS: 5
CAPACITY: 380 seated /1,000 standing
PRIVATE DINING: 380
CIVIL CEREMONIES: No
CUISINE: Flexible catering

MADDOX

A RESTAURANT, BAR & NIGHTCLUB

"Decadent but not showy, Maddox remains a popular spot to dine and dance."

3-5 Mill Street, London W1S 2AU
T: *020 7499 8113* W: *www.maddoxclub.com*

OPENING HOURS:
Wednesday to Saturday
9pm – 3am

GOOD FOR GOING OUT...
...for a night of dancing to top DJs with fashionable friends.
...for dinner with flash friends, before descending below ground to the slick nightclub.

GOOD FOR HOSTING...
...a sexy and sleek private event on a Sunday, Monday or Tuesday.
...a private table to impress friends and colleagues.

LOCATION: Mayfair
NEAREST TUBE: Oxford Circus
FUNCTION ROOMS: 4
CAPACITY: 80 seated / 352 standing
PRIVATE DINING: 20, 80
CIVIL CEREMONIES: No
CUISINE: Modern European

MADISON

A RESTAURANT

"Offering views over St Paul's Cathedral and the London skyline, and with a relaxed but stylish vibe, this is a unique roof terrace restaurant available to the public."

One New Change, London EC4M 9AF
T: *020 8305 3088* W: *www.madisonlondon.net*

OPENING HOURS:
Open daily
7am – 11pm

GOOD FOR GOING OUT...
...for breakfast with an early bird.
...for an informal lunch meeting with colleagues and clients.
...for an alfresco picnic with views.
...for a catch up glass of wine with a friend in the stylish and urban-cool bar.
...for a relaxed and low-key dinner with your boyfriend or girlfriend, in cool surroundings.

LOCATION: The City
NEAREST TUBE: St Paul's
FUNCTION ROOMS: 2
CAPACITY: 120 seated / 250 standing
PRIVATE DINING: 120
CIVIL CEREMONIES: Yes
CUISINE: British

MAGGIE'S
A NIGHTCLUB

"A 1980s themed boutique nightclub in Chelsea that pulls a fun-loving crowd every day of the week."

329 Fulham Road, London SW10 9QL
T: *020 7352 8512* W: *www.maggies-club.com*

OPENING HOURS:
Wednesday and Thursday / Friday and Saturday
10.30pm – 2:30am / 3:30am

GOOD FOR GOING OUT...
...for a dance to a myriad of eighties classics.
...for classic cocktails and dancing with a group of friends.
...if you're in fancy dress.
...with an eighties throwback.

GOOD FOR HOSTING...
...an all-out eighties themed birthday party for up to 180 people.
...an early evening drinks party with a carefree edge.

LOCATION: Chelsea
NEAREST TUBE: South Kensington
FUNCTION ROOMS: 1
CAPACITY: 180 standing
PRIVATE DINING: N/A
CIVIL CEREMONIES: No
CUISINE: N/A

MAHIKI
A NIGHTCLUB

"Leave your Heirs and Graces at home, just bring your sense of humour and your dancing shoes."

1 Dover St, London W1S 4LD
T: *020 7493 9529* W: *www.mahiki.com*

OPENING HOURS:
Monday to Friday
5:30pm – 3:30am
Saturday
7:30pm – 3:30am

GOOD FOR GOING OUT...
...for a night of quirky cocktails and dancing to the early hours with carefree friends.
...with a lover of tropical island life and mainstream music.

GOOD FOR HOSTING...
...a naughty night out with VIPs who favour discretion, in the secret private room.

LOCATION: Mayfair
NEAREST TUBE: Green Park
FUNCTION ROOMS: 2
CAPACITY: 350 standing
PRIVATE DINING: N/A
CIVIL CEREMONIES: No
CUISINE: Pan Asian / Bar snacks

THE MANDARIN ORIENTAL
A HOTEL

"Excelling in faultless service, The Mandarin Oriental offers a winning combination of restaurants, bars and private event spaces."

66 Knightsbridge, London SW1X 7LA
T: *020 7235 2000* W: *www.mandarinoriental.com / london*

GOOD FOR GOING OUT...
...for an informal but refined business coffee in the hotel's bar.
...for lunch with a glamorous friend in **Bar Boulud**, to take a break from shopping.
...for dinner with a burger-loving date at **Bar Boulud**.
...for a buzzy but sophisticated dinner with clients at **Bar Boulud**.

GOOD FOR HOSTING...
...a traditional and elegant intimate wedding or banquet in the beautiful surroundings of **The Loggia**.
...a large-scale wedding in **The Ballroom** with a drinks reception on **The Terrace** overlooking Hyde Park.

LOCATION: Knightsbridge
NEAREST TUBE: Knightsbridge
FUNCTION ROOMS: 7
CAPACITY: 250 seated / 400 standing
PRIVATE DINING: 30, 60, 120, 250
CIVIL CEREMONIES: Yes
CUISINE: British / French

MEWS OF MAYFAIR
A RESTAURANT & BAR

"Tucked away behind Bond Street, Mews of Mayfair pulls a sharply suited crowd of keen drinkers."

10 Lancashire Court, New Bond Street, London W1S 1EY
T: *020 7518 9395* W: *www.mewsofmayfair.com*

OPENING HOURS:
Sunday to Tuesday / Wednesday to Saturday
12pm – 11pm / 12pm – 1am

GOOD FOR GOING OUT...
...for after-work drinks with colleagues and friends, in the atmospheric cocktail bar.
...for a refined lunch or dinner with clients in the contemporary, chic restaurant.
...for after-dinner drinks in the basement lounge, where you can seek some privacy with a date in an alcove.

GOOD FOR HOSTING...
...a candlelit birthday dinner for up to 28 guests, in the unique, antique map-lined private dining room.
...a lunch with clients with a view of the chefs at work.

LOCATION: Mayfair
NEAREST TUBE: Bond Street
FUNCTION ROOMS: 5
CAPACITY: 150 seated / 350 standing
PRIVATE DINING: 16, 28, 70, 150
CIVIL CEREMONIES: No
CUISINE: Modern European

MIDDLE TEMPLE HALL
AN EVENT SPACE

"A magnificent and imposing Elizabethan Hall, Middle Temple is available for spectacular events throughout the year."

Middle Temple Lane, London EC4Y 9AT
T: *0844 858 0673* W: *www.middletemplehall.org.uk*

OPENING HOURS:
Open daily for events and private hire
7am – 11pm

GOOD FOR HOSTING...
...a dramatic and impressive banquet in the wood-paneled
    Hall for up to 500 people.
...a traditional wedding ceremony for up to 75 people.
...an idyllic Champagne reception in the gardens for up
    to 700 people.

LOCATION: The City
NEAREST TUBE: Temple
FUNCTION ROOMS: 4
CAPACITY: 500 seated
PRIVATE DINING: N/A
CIVIL CEREMONIES: Yes
CUISINE: Flexible catering

MIN JIANG
A RESTAURANT

"Serving critically acclaimed Chinese food, Min Jiang is a unique offering in Kensington. Go during daylight to really enjoy the view over the park."

2-24 Kensington High Street, London W8 4PT
T: *020 7361 1988* W: *www.minjiang.co.uk*

OPENING HOURS:
Open daily
12pm – 3pm; 6pm – 10:30pm

GOOD FOR GOING OUT...
...for a celebratory lunch with colleagues and clients.
...for a birthday dinner, to enjoy fine Chinese cuisine
    with your family.

GOOD FOR HOSTING...
...an intimate dinner in the private dining room with up
    to 20 colleagues and clients after early-evening aperitifs
    in the bar.

LOCATION: Kensington
NEAREST TUBE: High St Kensington
FUNCTION ROOMS: 1
CAPACITY: 80 seated
PRIVATE DINING: 20, 80
CIVIL CEREMONIES: No
CUISINE: Chinese

LOCATION:	The City
NEAREST TUBE:	Bank
FUNCTION ROOMS:	3
CAPACITY:	90 seated / 300 standing
PRIVATE DINING:	60, 90
CIVIL CEREMONIES:	Yes
CUISINE:	Indian

MINT LEAF LOUNGE & RESTAURANT
A RESTAURANT & BAR

"Mint Leaf Lounge and Restaurant serves innovative Indian cuisine and boasts one of the longest cocktail bars in the City."

12 Angel Court, London EC2R 7HB
T: *020 7600 0992* W: *www.mintleaflounge.com*

GOOD FOR GOING OUT...

...for cocktails with colleagues or friends, to enjoy from the comfort of a booth in the bar.

...throughout the day to enjoy small bites and platters.

...for lunch with clients in the elegant and contemporary restaurant.

...with a group of up to 4 people to experience the **Chef's Table** and tasting menu.

GOOD FOR HOSTING...

...a relaxed but sophisticated drinks party for up to 60 colleagues and clients in the bar and lounge.

...a stylish drinks and canapé reception in the **Mezzanine Champagne Bar**.

LOCATION:	Piccadilly
NEAREST TUBE:	Piccadilly Circus
FUNCTION ROOMS:	2
CAPACITY:	240 seated / 450 standing
PRIVATE DINING:	65, 240
CIVIL CEREMONIES:	Yes
CUISINE:	Indian

MINT LEAF RESTAURANT & BAR
A RESTAURANT & BAR

"Smart and sophisticated, Mint Leaf in Piccadilly serves modern Indian cuisine in an atmospheric, contemporary setting."

Suffolk Place, London SW1Y 4HX
T: *020 7930 9020* W: *www.mintleafrestaurant.com*

OPENING HOURS:
Monday to Friday / Saturday and Sunday
12pm – 3pm; 5:30pm – 11pm / 5:30pm – 10:30pm

GOOD FOR GOING OUT...

...for an indulgent and atmospheric client lunch or dinner.

...with colleagues and clients for cocktails and light bites throughout the evening.

...for dinner followed by drinks with live DJ sets in the cocktail lounge with a date, on a Friday or Saturday night.

GOOD FOR HOSTING...

...a fashion show or launch party with cocktail reception and sit down dinner.

...a cocktail masterclass for up to 20 guests.

...a dinner for up to 65 people in the sleek private dining room.

MORTON'S
A PRIVATE MEMBERS' CLUB

"Morton's is a relaxed but elegant members' club and each floor is available for private hire at certain times when not open to members."

28 Berkeley Square, London W1J 6EN
T: *020 7499 0363* W: *www.mortonsclub.com*

OPENING HOURS:
Monday to Friday / Saturday
7:30am – 3am / 5pm – 3am

GOOD FOR GOING OUT...
...if you're lucky enough to be a member.

GOOD FOR HOSTING...
...a birthday dinner with up to 48 friends in an exclusive home-from-home setting with a wine list of 1,700 bins to choose from.
...a business breakfast and presentation overlooking Berkeley Square.
...a wedding breakfast in the beautiful dining room on a Saturday afternoon.
...a Christmas drinks party with dancing before 10pm any night or until 3am on Mondays and Tuesdays.

LOCATION: Mayfair
NEAREST TUBE: Bond Street
FUNCTION ROOMS: 4
CAPACITY: 48 seated / 70 standing
PRIVATE DINING: 24, 48
CIVIL CEREMONIES: No
CUISINE: French / Italian / Patisserie

MOVIDA
A NIGHTCLUB

"Movida remains one of the biggest and best clubs in Central London, pulling an eclectic group of party-goers."

8-9 Argyll Street, London W1F 7TF
T: *020 7734 5776* W: *www.movida-london.com*

OPENING HOURS:
Wednesday to Saturday
10:30pm – 4am

GOOD FOR GOING OUT...
...to see cutting-edge DJs from around the world.
...to be seen amongst celebrities and beautiful people.
...to dance all night to a great sound system.

GOOD FOR HOSTING...
...an early evening canapé party in one section of the venue before dancing the night away when the club opens.
...an impressive launch party throughout the whole venue.
...a fashion show at any time of day.
...a party anywhere, but bringing in Movida's pop-up bar and mixologists to add some wow factor.

LOCATION: West End
NEAREST TUBE: Oxford Circus
FUNCTION ROOMS: 3
CAPACITY: 400 standing
PRIVATE DINING: N/A
CIVIL CEREMONIES: No
CUISINE: N/A

NOBU LONDON
A RESTAURANT

"Nobuyuki Matsuhisa's first restaurant in Europe, Nobu London offers a restaurant and a sushi bar complete with views across Hyde Park."

19 Old Park Lane, London W1K 1LB
T: *020 7447 4747* W: *www.noburestaurants.com*

OPENING HOURS:
Monday to Friday / Saturday / Sunday
12pm – 2:15pm / 2:30pm / 2:30pm;
6pm – 11pm / 11pm / 10pm

GOOD FOR GOING OUT...
...for exquisite Japanese cuisine in buzzy but sophisticated surroundings, with clients you want to impress.
...for an intimate date with a lover of sushi.

GOOD FOR HOSTING...
...an indulgent, memorable and unique private dinner in one of Nobu's principal private dining spaces: a suite in the **May Fair Hotel**.
...a Michelin-starred Japanese feast in any location of your choice, with **Nobu's Event Catering** service.

LOCATION: Mayfair
NEAREST TUBE: Hyde Park Corner
FUNCTION ROOMS: 2
CAPACITY: 200 seated / 400 standing
PRIVATE DINING: 50, 200
CIVIL CEREMONIES: No
CUISINE: Japanese

NUMBER SIXTEEN
A HOTEL

"With its own tree-filled private garden and all the facilities expected of a luxury hotel, Number Sixteen is a hidden gem."

16 Sumner Place, London SW7 3EG
T: *020 7589 5232* W: *www.firmdale.com*

GOOD FOR GOING OUT...
...with friends for afternoon tea in **The Conservatory** on a sunny day.
...for afternoon tea in **The Library** to get cosy on a rainy afternoon.

GOOD FOR HOSTING...
...an intimate wedding in the tree-filled garden and **Conservatory**.
...an atmospheric private dinner in **The Conservatory**.

LOCATION: South Kensington
NEAREST TUBE: South Kensington
FUNCTION ROOMS: 1
CAPACITY: 10 seated / 50 standing
PRIVATE DINING: 10
CIVIL CEREMONIES: Yes
CUISINE: British / Afternoon Tea

OLD BILLINGSGATE
AN EVENT SPACE

"Renowned in the City for its ability to transform any event into a spectacular one, Old Billingsgate is a unique and glittering venue."

1 Old Billingsgate Walk, 16 Lower Thames Street,
London EC3R 6DX
T: *020 7283 2800* W: *www.oldbillingsgate.co.uk*

OPENING HOURS:
Open daily for events and private hire

GOOD FOR HOSTING...

...a sexy, creative and impressive launch party or
fashion show.

...a corporate but cool and memorable Christmas party
with live entertainment, a sit down dinner and dancing.

...an awards ceremony or conference which requires
some no-holds-barred wow factor.

LOCATION: The City
NEAREST TUBE: Monument
FUNCTION ROOMS: 3
CAPACITY: 1,200 seated / 2,400 standing
PRIVATE DINING: N/A
CIVIL CEREMONIES: No
CUISINE: Flexible catering

THE OLD QUEEN'S HEAD
A PUB

"Don your Converse and dance to live bands and DJs in this popular pub where relaxed rustic meets urban cool."

44 Essex Road, London N1 8LN
T: *020 7354 9993* W: *www.theoldqueenshead.com*

OPENING HOURS:
Sunday to Wednesday / Thursday / Friday and Saturday
12pm – 12am / 12pm – 1am / 12pm – 2am

GOOD FOR GOING OUT...

...to check out cool new bands and DJs in an intimate
party environment.

...on a Sunday evening when you're not quite ready for
the weekend to be over.

GOOD FOR HOSTING...

...a birthday party with a group of friends when you want
everyone to get stuck in.

...a launch party when you're looking for some shabby-chic,
urban edge.

LOCATION: Angel
NEAREST TUBE: Angel
FUNCTION ROOMS: 2
CAPACITY: 100 seated / 170 standing
PRIVATE DINING: 60, 100
CIVIL CEREMONIES: No
CUISINE: Pub fare

REVIEW ONLINE

ONE ALDWYCH
A HOTEL

"With a bar, two restaurants, screening room, spa and other event spaces available, this hotel has something to suit all needs, at all times of the day."

1 Aldwych, London WC2B 4BZ
T: *020 7300 0700* W: *www.onealdwych.com*

GOOD FOR GOING OUT...

...for a good value pre- or post-theatre fixed menu in ***Axis***, with friends.

...for a relaxed but refined business breakfast in ***Indigo***.

...for an informal but sophisticated drink with a client in ***The Lobby Bar***.

...for a date to eat in ***Axis*** and watch a movie in the ***Screening Room***.

GOOD FOR HOSTING...

...a screening or presentation that requires full multimedia services in comfortable surroundings.

...cookery school and wine-tasting events with colleagues and clients in a chic setting.

...a formal private lunch or dinner with clients.

LOCATION: West End
NEAREST TUBE: Covent Garden
FUNCTION ROOMS: 6
CAPACITY: 80 seated / 180 standing
PRIVATE DINING: 80
CIVIL CEREMONIES: Yes
CUISINE: British

OPERA TAVERN
A RESTAURANT

"Fear not – there is no need to sing for your heavenly supper at this tapas bar and restaurant in Covent Garden."

23 Catherine Street, London WC2B 515
T: *020 7836 3680* W: *www.operatavern.co.uk*

OPENING HOURS:
Monday to Saturday
12pm – 11:30pm
Sunday
12pm – 3pm

GOOD FOR GOING OUT...

...on a date to enjoy delectable tapas in the cosy and buzzy, no-reservations downstairs restaurant.

...for a pre-opera or pre-theatre dinner with your parents in the first floor restaurant.

...for a glass of wine at the bar, to have a catch up with a friend over some small plates of tapas.

LOCATION: Covent Garden
NEAREST TUBE: Covent Garden
FUNCTION ROOMS: 1
CAPACITY: 40 seated
PRIVATE DINING: 40
CIVIL CEREMONIES: No
CUISINE: Tapas

THE ORANGE
A PUBLIC HOUSE & HOTEL

"The Orange is a destination haunt for local residents, families, the young, and the old from neighbouring Chelsea, Belgravia and Pimlico."

37 Pimlico Road, London SW1W 8NE
T: *020 7881 9844* W: *www.theorange.co.uk*

OPENING HOURS:
Monday to Thursday / Friday and Saturday / Sunday
8am – 11:30pm / 8am – 12am / 8am – 10:30pm

GOOD FOR GOING OUT...
...for an informal business breakfast.
...for a catch up with friends in a charming and rustic setting.
...for a relaxed date to have a wood-fired pizza in a comfortable setting.

GOOD FOR HOSTING...
...a relaxed but buzzy and chic birthday drinks party with friends.
...an informal lunch meeting with colleagues for a brainstorm.
...a candlelit dinner party for friends and family.

LOCATION: Pimlico
NEAREST TUBE: Sloane Square
FUNCTION ROOMS: 5
CAPACITY: 70 seated / 120 standing
PRIVATE DINING: 12, 18, 25, 40, 70
CIVIL CEREMONIES: No
CUISINE: British / European

OXO TOWER
A RESTAURANT & BAR

"With spectacular views, The Oxo Tower is a fantastic spot, serving some of the best food on the South Bank."

Barge House Street, South Bank, London SE1 9PH
T: *020 7803 3888* W: *www.harveynichols.com*

OPENING HOURS:
Monday to Friday / Saturday / Sunday
12pm – 2:30pm / 12pm – 2:30pm / 12pm – 3pm;
6pm – 11pm / 5:30pm – 11pm / 6:30pm – 10pm

GOOD FOR GOING OUT...
...for a catch up drink in the bar with a friend, to enjoy a unique and stylishly contemporary setting.
...for an informal but sophisticated lunch in the *brasserie*.
...for a celebratory dinner with your family in the *restaurant*.
...for alfresco dining on the *terrace* in the Summer months with spectacular river views.

GOOD FOR HOSTING...
...a memorable Christmas party for colleagues and clients.
...a launch party or exhibition in a contemporary space.

LOCATION: Southbank
NEAREST TUBE: Waterloo
FUNCTION ROOMS: 3
CAPACITY: 320 seated / 700 standing
PRIVATE DINING: 65, 150, 320
CIVIL CEREMONIES: Yes
CUISINE: Modern European

LOCATION:	Belgravia
NEAREST TUBE:	Knightsbridge
FUNCTION ROOMS:	2
CAPACITY:	120 seated / 150 standing
PRIVATE DINING:	50, 120
CIVIL CEREMONIES:	No
CUISINE:	American / Steak

THE PALM
A RESTAURANT

"It may be pricey but The Palm offers fantastic steak in a space that's packed with personality."

1 Pont St, London SW1X 9EJ
T: *020 7201 0710* W: *www.thepalm.com /london*

OPENING HOURS:
Monday to Friday
6pm – 11pm
Saturday / Sunday
12pm – 5pm; 5pm – 11pm / 10pm

GOOD FOR GOING OUT...
...with lovers of American ways.
...for a relaxed lunch in characterful surroundings, with clients who have a penchant for steak.

GOOD FOR HOSTING...
...an indulgent dinner party with clients, in a quirky but sophisticated setting.
...a dinner in the ***Palm Private Dining Room*** to celebrate a special occasion.

LOCATION:	Knightsbridge
NEAREST TUBE:	Knightsbridge
FUNCTION ROOMS:	3
CAPACITY:	46 seated / 80 standing
PRIVATE DINING:	14, 20, 46
CIVIL CEREMONIES:	No
CUISINE:	British

THE PANTECHNICON
A PUBLIC HOUSE

"Understated but atmospheric, relaxed but refined, this pub-style restaurant will keep a boys' working lunch going till evening."

10 Motcomb Street, London SW1X 8LA
T: *020 7730 6074* W: *www.thepantechnicon.com*

OPENING HOURS:
Monday to Friday
12pm – 11pm
Saturday / Sunday
9am – 11pm; 9am – 10:30pm

GOOD FOR GOING OUT...
...for a relaxed but stylish dinner date in buzzy and welcoming surroundings, on the ground floor (no reservations).
...for a refined client lunch in traditional British surroundings, on the first floor.

GOOD FOR HOSTING...
...a client dinner in a townhouse-style private dining room.
...a low-key candlelit birthday dinner with friends and family.

PARADISE
BY WAY OF KENSAL GREEN
A GASTRO PUB

"Quirky, eclectic, shabby but chic, this hedonist's heaven pulls huge crowds every week."

19 Kilburn Lane, London W10 4AE
T: *020 8969 0098* W: *www.theparadise.co.uk*

OPENING HOURS:
Monday to Wednesday / Thursday / Friday
4pm – 12am / 4pm – 1am / 4pm – 2am
Saturday / Sunday
12pm – 2am / 12pm – 12am

GOOD FOR GOING OUT...
...for a casual but fun dinner date before cocktails in the bar.
...for dinner with a group, before dancing the night away.
...for Sunday lunch with friends and a bottle of red.

GOOD FOR HOSTING...
...a fun and intimate dinner in a private dining room before dancing till the early hours.
...a party with live music and a good outside space.
...a party for up to 20 friends in the *Private Karaoke Room*.

LOCATION: Kensal Green
NEAREST TUBE: Kensal Green / Rise
FUNCTION ROOMS: 5
CAPACITY: 70 seated / 500 standing
PRIVATE DINING: 16, 20, 70
CIVIL CEREMONIES: Yes
CUISINE: British

PIZZA EAST
A RESTAURANT & EVENT SPACE

"Fun, vibrant, relaxed and buzzing, Pizza East is the coolest place for pizza in town."

56 Shoreditch High Street, London E1
T: *020 7729 1888* W: *www.pizzaeast.com / london*

OPENING HOURS:
Monday to Wednesday / Thursday / Friday
12pm – 12am / 12pm – 1am / 12pm – 2am
Saturday / Sunday
10am – 2am / 10am – 12am

GOOD FOR GOING OUT...
...for a fun dinner with friends to unwind and relax.
...for dinner with a big group to celebrate a birthday.

GOOD FOR HOSTING...
...a trendy launch party in *Concrete* on the lower ground floor, for a rustic, warehouse vibe.
...a Christmas party for trendy-types in *Concrete*, with live music and dancing.

LOCATION: Shoreditch
NEAREST TUBE: Shoreditch High St
FUNCTION ROOMS: 1
CAPACITY: 18 seated
PRIVATE DINING: 18
CIVIL CEREMONIES: No
CUISINE: Pizza / Italian

REVIEW ONLINE

POLPO
A RESTAURANT & BAR

"You can't book ahead but there's a reason why people are prepared to queue."

41 Beak Street, London W1F 9SB
T: *020 7734 4479* W: *www.polpo.co.uk*

OPENING HOURS:
Monday to Saturday
12pm – 3pm; 5:30pm – 11pm
Sunday
12pm – 4pm

GOOD FOR GOING OUT…
…on an impromptu date, to a rustic and low-lit, intimate space, to share small plates of tapas.
…for a relaxed catch up with a friend over Prosecco and polpette.

LOCATION: Soho
NEAREST TUBE: Piccadilly Circus
FUNCTION ROOMS: N/A
CAPACITY: N/A
PRIVATE DINING: N/A
CIVIL CEREMONIES: No
CUISINE: Italian

PORTRAIT RESTAURANT, NATIONAL PORTRAIT GALLERY
A RESTAURANT

"The view from this cultural institution gives you a superior standpoint in more ways than one."

St Martin's Place, London WC2H 0HE
T: *020 7312 2490* W: *searcys.co.uk/national-portrait-gallery*

OPENING HOURS:
Open daily
10am – 11:15am; 11:45am – 2:45pm; 3:30pm – 4:45pm;
5:30pm – 8:30pm (Thursday to Saturday only)

GOOD FOR GOING OUT…
…for a delicious but light breakfast to catch up with a friend before visiting the gallery.
…for a relaxed but refined catch up lunch with your parents.
…for afternoon tea when you need sustenance for getting round exhibitions.
…for dinner with a date you want to impress with great views and a unique venue.

LOCATION: West End
NEAREST TUBE: Charing Cross
FUNCTION ROOMS: 1
CAPACITY: 80 seated / 200 standing
PRIVATE DINING: N/A
CIVIL CEREMONIES: No
CUISINE: British / Afternoon Tea

PROUD CABARET
A RESTAURANT, BAR & LIVE ENTERTAINMENT VENUE

"Modeled on a 1920s speakeasy, Proud Cabaret offers fine dining and live entertainment in sexy and opulent surroundings in the City."

No.1 Mark Lane, London EC3R 7AH
T: *020 7283 1940* W: *www.proudcabaret.com*

OPENING HOURS:
Wednesday and Thursday
6:30pm – 2am
Friday and Saturday
6:30pm – 3am

GOOD FOR GOING OUT...
...for dinner with friends when you're looking for something a little bit different.
...with a lover of burlesque and retro supper clubs.
...on a date to enjoy cocktails and light bites from the bar menu as you watch the evening's entertainment unfold.

GOOD FOR HOSTING...
...a private and decadent event with dinner and drinks, with live performances to impress and entertain guests.

LOCATION: The City
NEAREST TUBE: Monument
FUNCTION ROOMS: 1
CAPACITY: 240 seated / 330 standing
PRIVATE DINING: 240
CIVIL CEREMONIES: No
CUISINE: British

PROUD2
A LIVE ENTERTAINMENT VENUE

"Proud2 has completely redesigned the space that was Matter in The O2, to create a visual spectacle."

The O2, Peninsula Square, London SE10 0DX
T: *020 8463 3070* W: *www.proud2.com*

OPENING HOURS:
Open daily for private hire and events.

GOOD FOR GOING OUT...
...for unique 'experience clubbing'.
...for a decadent and glamorous night out to remember, with circus-themed productions and eclectic entertainment.

GOOD FOR HOSTING...
...a party in a **Party Booth** on the 3rd floor for up to 50 friends, to include free entry for all before 10pm.
...an entertaining night out with clients in a **VIP Booth**.
...an eye-popping extravaganza for up to 3,500 people, incorporating an unrivaled sound system and an entertainment stage.

LOCATION: Greenwich
NEAREST TUBE: North Greenwich
FUNCTION ROOMS: 5
CAPACITY: 300 seated / 3,500 standing
PRIVATE DINING: N/A
CIVIL CEREMONIES: Yes
CUISINE: N/A

THE PROVIDORES & TAPA ROOM
A RESTAURANT

*"Located on chic Marylebone High Street,
The Providores and Tapa Room serve exemplary
fusion cuisine and one of the best coffees in town."*

109 Marylebone High Street, London W1U 4RX
T: *020 7935 6175* W: *www.theprovidores.co.uk*

OPENING HOURS:
Monday to Friday / Saturday / Sunday
9am – 10:30pm / 10am – 10:30pm / 10am – 10pm

GOOD FOR GOING OUT...
...for a delectable breakfast or brunch with your girlfriend
or boyfriend.
...for an informal lunch meeting with someone stylish in
the ***Tapa Room*** – the all day café and bar.
...for an intimate and relaxed dinner date to enjoy small
sharer plates in the more formal first floor restaurant.
...with someone Antipodean.

LOCATION: Marylebone
NEAREST TUBE: Bond Street
FUNCTION ROOMS: 1
CAPACITY: 40 seated
PRIVATE DINING: 40
CIVIL CEREMONIES: No
CUISINE: Small plates / Fusion

PUBLIC
A NIGHTCLUB

*"PUBLIC is 5000 square feet of virgin industrial
glam – a clubbing heaven where London's finest
dress up, drink up and get down."*

533 Kings Road, London SW10 0TZ
T: *020 7751 4400* W: *www.public.uk.com*

OPENING HOURS:
Thursday to Saturday
10pm – 3am

GOOD FOR GOING OUT...
...for a night of dancing amongst a fun-loving and glamorous
Chelsea set in a New York-style industrial space.
...and taking a table in the bar area to enjoy chatting in
the booths before hitting the dancefloor.

GOOD FOR HOSTING...
...a night out with cool colleagues and clients in the
VIP room.
...a launch party or exhibition in Public's rustic and raw
private event space, for a funky warehouse feel.

LOCATION: Chelsea
NEAREST TUBE: Fulham Broadway
FUNCTION ROOMS: 2
CAPACITY: 450 standing
PRIVATE DINING: N/A
CIVIL CEREMONIES: No
CUISINE: N/A

QUINTESSENTIALLY SOHO AT THE HOUSE OF ST BARNABAS

AN EVENT SPACE

"A charitable and charming event space in the heart of Soho that is available for private hire."

1 Greek Street, London W1D 4NQ
T: *020 7437 1894*
W: *www.hosb.org.uk / www.quintessentiallysoho.com*

OPENING HOURS:
Open daily for events and private hire

GOOD FOR GOING OUT...
...if you're lucky enough to be a member.

GOOD FOR HOSTING...
...a Champagne and canapé party in the beautiful Georgian
 style rooms, where traditional features are complemented
 with modern art to create a unique and glamorous space.
...a summer party in the private garden courtyard.

LOCATION: Soho
NEAREST TUBE: Tottenham Court Rd
FUNCTION ROOMS: 8
CAPACITY: 50 seated / 300 standing
PRIVATE DINING: N/A
CIVIL CEREMONIES: No
CUISINE: Flexible catering

QUO VADIS

A RESTAURANT & BAR

*"From the two brothers who also brought us
Barrafina and Fino, this is a sophisticated
destination on Dean Street."*

26-29 Dean Street, London W1D 3LL
T: *020 7437 9585* W: *www.quovadissoho.co.uk*

OPENING HOURS:
Monday to Saturday
12pm – 2:45pm; 5:30pm – 10:45pm

GOOD FOR GOING OUT...
...for an after-work drink in the small but stylish ground
 floor bar.
...for a pre-theatre dinner with a group of friends.

GOOD FOR HOSTING...
...a relaxed meeting with clients in an elegant private
 dining room set within the members' club.

LOCATION: Soho
NEAREST TUBE: Tottenham Court Rd
FUNCTION ROOMS: 3
CAPACITY: 36 seated / 80 standing
PRIVATE DINING: 12, 24, 36
CIVIL CEREMONIES: No
CUISINE: British

REVIEW ONLINE

RAFFLES
A NIGHTCLUB

"Raffles keeps going till quite late so with a license till 5am this is the place for fun-loving night owls."

287 Kings Road, London SW3 5EW
T: *020 7351 4964* W: *www.raffleschelsea.com*

OPENING HOURS:
Wednesday to Saturday
10pm – 5am

GOOD FOR GOING OUT...
...dancing with an exhibitionist friend who will want to dance on the podium, in this intimate boutique club.
...with a group of friends to enjoy booth seating and a flashing dance floor.
...with an insomniac.

GOOD FOR HOSTING...
...after parties where discretion is key.
...poker nights in the privacy of the first floor private room and bar.

LOCATION: Chelsea
NEAREST TUBE: South Kensington
FUNCTION ROOMS: 2
CAPACITY: 220 standing
PRIVATE DINING: N/A
CIVIL CEREMONIES: No
CUISINE: N/A

REVIEW ONLINE

REDHOOK
A RESTAURANT & BAR

"With seafood, steak, cocktails and oysters on the menu, you'll fall (red)hook, line and sinker."

89 Turnmill Street, London EC1M 5QU
T: *020 7065 6800* W: *www.redhooklondon.com*

OPENING HOURS:
Open daily
10am – 12am

GOOD FOR GOING OUT...
...for an informal working lunch with a client.
...for after-work drinks at the bar with colleagues, to unwind in the relaxed and comfortable setting.
...for dinner with with a group of friends in buzzy surroundings.

GOOD FOR HOSTING...
...a birthday dinner with a group of friends in the atmospheric private room that looks over the restaurant.

LOCATION: The City
NEAREST TUBE: Farringdon
FUNCTION ROOMS: 1
CAPACITY: 64 seated / 150 standing
PRIVATE DINING: 14, 64
CIVIL CEREMONIES: No
CUISINE: Steak / Seafood / American

THE RITZ
A HOTEL

"The Ritz is one of the most traditionally British and lavish places to be in central London."

150 Piccadilly, London W1J 9BR
T: *020 7493 8181* W: *www.theritzlondon.com*

OPENING HOURS:
Monday to Saturday / Sunday
Restaurant: 7am – 10:30am; 12:30pm – 2pm; 5:30pm – 10pm /
8am – 10:30am; 12:30pm – 2pm; 7pm – 10:30pm
Afternoon Tea: 11:30am – 7:30pm

GOOD FOR GOING OUT...
...for a traditional and renowned afternoon tea with your
  mother to mark a special occasion.
...for drinks and a light bite in the lavish art deco **Rivoli
  Bar**, for a date with a touch of grandeur.
...for dinner to mark a special occasion with your family.

GOOD FOR HOSTING...
...a small, intimate and personal wedding for close friends
  and family.
...a grand and lavish banquet for clients you wish to impress.

LOCATION: Mayfair
NEAREST TUBE: Green Park
FUNCTION ROOMS: 6
CAPACITY: 60 seated / 120 standing
PRIVATE DINING: 16, 24, 30, 60
CIVIL CEREMONIES: Yes
CUISINE: British

RIVER CAFÉ
A RESTAURANT

"It comes at a price but Italian food in this setting is worth forking out for."

Thames Wharf, Rainville Road, London W6 9HA
T: *020 7386 4200* W: *www.rivercafe.co.uk*

OPENING HOURS:
Monday to Thursday / Friday
12:30pm – 2:15pm; 7pm – 9pm / 9:15pm
Saturday / Sunday
12:30pm – 2:30 / 3pm; 7pm – 9:15pm (closed Sunday dinner)

GOOD FOR GOING OUT...
...for an indulgent lunch with a foodie friend.
...for a glamorous lunch with girlfriends on the alfresco
  terrace in the Summer months.
...for a celebratory dinner with friends in a contemporary
  but stylish setting.

GOOD FOR HOSTING...
...a private lunch for up to 18 clients with views of the
  kitchen and the terrace.

LOCATION: Hammersmith
NEAREST TUBE: Hammersmith
FUNCTION ROOMS: 1
CAPACITY: 18 seated
PRIVATE DINING: 18
CIVIL CEREMONIES: No
CUISINE: Italian

ROAST

A RESTAURANT

"Located over Borough Market, Roast serves honest, gutsy, hearty and delicious food using only the finest seasonal produce."

Borough Market, Stoney Street, London SE1 1TL
T: 0845 034 7300 W: www.roast-restaurant.com

OPENING HOURS:

Monday and Tuesday / Wednesday to Friday
7am – 11am; 12pm – 2:45pm / 3:45; 5:30pm – 10:30pm
Saturday / Sunday
8am – 11:30am; 12.15pm – 3:45pm; 6pm – 10:30pm / 11:30am – 6pm

GOOD FOR GOING OUT...

...for a substantial Saturday brunch with your family.
...for a relaxed working lunch with clients in light and airy surroundings.
...for a sophisticated dinner with colleagues following cocktails in the bar with a live pianist.

GOOD FOR HOSTING...

...a drinks party for up to 220 people in an impressive space.

LOCATION: Borough
NEAREST TUBE: London Bridge
FUNCTION ROOMS: 1
CAPACITY: 120 seated / 220 standing
PRIVATE DINING: 120
CIVIL CEREMONIES: Yes
CUISINE: British

ROKA

A RESTAURANT & BAR

"Roka serves great food in a great atmosphere with a buzzing bar downstairs. Counter-dine at the central Robata grill for the full experience."

37 Charlotte Street, London W1T 1RR
T: 020 7580 6464 W: www.rokarestaurant.com

OPENING HOURS:

Monday to Friday
12pm – 3:30pm; 5:30pm – 11:30pm
Saturday / Sunday
12:30pm – 3:30pm; 5:30pm – 11:30pm / 10:30pm

GOOD FOR GOING OUT...

...on a dinner date with someone glamorous, starting with a drink in the sexy ***Shochu Lounge***.
...for informal but sophisticated after-work drinks with a client.
...with a sushi lover for lunch or dinner, and sitting at the bar to see the chefs at work.

LOCATION: Fitzrovia
NEAREST TUBE: Goodge Street
FUNCTION ROOMS: 1
CAPACITY: 88 seated
PRIVATE DINING: 88
CIVIL CEREMONIES: No
CUISINE: Japanese

THE ROOF GARDENS & BABYLON

A NIGHTCLUB & RESTAURANT

"It doesn't matter how many times you've been – this rooftop garden remains one of the most exciting spaces in London."

6th Floor, 99 Kensington High Street, London W8 5SA
T: *020 7937 7994* W: *www.roofgardens.virgin.com*

OPENING HOURS:
Open daily
Babylon: 12pm – 3pm; 7 – 10:30pm
Roof Gardens: 10pm – 3am (Friday and Saturday only)

GOOD FOR GOING OUT...
...for supper at **Babylon** with a date, before cocktails on the roof and dancing in the club.
...for a night of dancing with friends.

GOOD FOR HOSTING...
...a Summer drinks party with wow factor.
...a Winter wonderland-themed Christmas party for colleagues and clients.

LOCATION: Kensington
NEAREST TUBE: High St Kensington
FUNCTION ROOMS: 3
CAPACITY: 180 seated / 500 standing
PRIVATE DINING: 12, 28, 180
CIVIL CEREMONIES: Yes
CUISINE: British

SALT YARD

A RESTAURANT

"With delicious charcuterie, tapas, wine and snacks on offer, The Salt Yard is worthy of its awards."

54 Goodge Street, London W1T 4NA
T: *020 7637 0657* W: *www.saltyard.co.uk*

OPENING HOURS:
Open daily
12pm – 11pm

GOOD FOR GOING OUT...
...for a light lunch in a chic setting.
...for an after-work catch up with a friend over drinks and bar snacks.
...on a low-key but romantic date to enjoy sharing delicious plates of tapas.

GOOD FOR HOSTING...
...a private dinner with an intimate feel for up to 40 people.

LOCATION: Fitzrovia
NEAREST TUBE: Goodge Street
FUNCTION ROOMS: 1
CAPACITY: 40 seated
PRIVATE DINING: 40
CIVIL CEREMONIES: No
CUISINE: Tapas

SANCTUM SOHO HOTEL
A HOTEL

"A roof garden in Central London with bar and alfresco hydro spa? Entertain here and your reputation will be made."

20 Warwick Street, London W1B 5NF
T: *020 7292 6100* W: *www.sanctumsoho.com*

OPENING HOURS:
Open daily
Restaurant: 6:30am – 11am; 12pm – 3pm; 6pm – 11pm
Bar: 10am – 11pm / 10am – 12am (Thursday to Saturday)

GOOD FOR GOING OUT...
...for after-work drinks with colleagues at **No. 20** before enjoying a low-key dinner in the restaurant.

GOOD FOR HOSTING...
...a screening for up to 45 clients in the decadent **Cinema Room**, complete with its own bar.
...a relaxed but vibrant birthday drinks party on the **Roof**, with the alfresco hydrospa for when things heat up.

LOCATION: Soho
NEAREST TUBE: Piccadilly Circus
FUNCTION ROOMS: 3
CAPACITY: 70 seated / 120 standing
PRIVATE DINING: 70
CIVIL CEREMONIES: No
CUISINE: British / Afternoon Tea

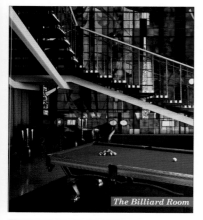

The Billiard Room

SANDERSON
A HOTEL

"Sanderson is a five star luxury hotel offering a stylish bar and restaurant in a beautifully and intriguingly designed space."

50 Berners Street, London W1T 3NG
T: *020 7300 1400* W: *www.sandersonlondon.com*

GOOD FOR GOING OUT...
...for pre- and post-dinner drinks in the stylish **Long Bar** with fashionable friends or clients.
...for cocktails in **The Courtyard** surrounded by a lush oasis of trees, flowers and fountains, to impress an out-of-towner.
...for dinner in the elegant minimalist **Suka** with a lover of Malaysian cuisine.

GOOD FOR HOSTING...
...a corporate drinks party in **The Billiard Room** with a speaker.
...a lavish launch party in **The Courtyard Garden**.
...a sexy cocktail party in **The Purple Bar**.

LOCATION: Fitzrovia
NEAREST TUBE: Goodge Street
FUNCTION ROOMS: 4
CAPACITY: 40 seated / 80 standing
PRIVATE DINING: 22, 40
CIVIL CEREMONIES: No
CUISINE: Malaysian / Afternoon Tea

THE SAVOY
A HOTEL

"Following the much-talked-about £100million restoration, the iconic Savoy once again takes its place amongst London's most glamorous five star hotels."

Strand, London WC2R 0EU
T: *020 7836 4343* W: *www.the-savoy.com*

GOOD FOR GOING OUT...

...for modern French cuisine in the elegant art deco **River Restaurant**, with views over the sparkling River Thames.
...for lunch with clients at the **Savoy Grill**.
...with a glamorous lover of Champagne in **The Beaufort Bar**.

GOOD FOR HOSTING...

...a wedding (grand or intimate) in one of nine licensed rooms.
...a meeting for refined clients in a formal private dining room.
...a dinner to mark a special occasion for up to 12 guests in the **River Restaurant**, overlooking the Thames.

LOCATION: The Strand
NEAREST TUBE: Charing Cross
FUNCTION ROOMS: 6
CAPACITY: 50 seated / 80 standing
PRIVATE DINING: 10, 12, 18, 24, 30, 50
CIVIL CEREMONIES: Yes
CUISINE: British / French

SCOTT'S
A RESTAURANT

"A favourite with the Mayfair set, fish lovers and celebrities alike."

20 Mount Street, London W1K 2HE
T: *020 7495 7309* W: *www.scotts-restaurant.com*

OPENING HOURS:
Monday to Saturday
12pm – 10:30pm
Sunday
12pm – 10pm

GOOD FOR GOING OUT...

...for lunch with clients you want to impress in one of London's consistently popular hotspots.
...for lunch with a fashionista before hitting Bond Street.
...for a date with someone glamorous and sociable.

GOOD FOR HOSTING...

...a candlelit dinner for up to 40 fun-loving clients in the below ground private dining room.

LOCATION: Mayfair
NEAREST TUBE: Bond Street
FUNCTION ROOMS: 1
CAPACITY: 40 seated / 50 standing
PRIVATE DINING: 40
CIVIL CEREMONIES: No
CUISINE: British / Seafood

SERPENTINE GALLERY
A GALLERY

"Rightfully named by The Observer as the most beautiful gallery in London."

Kensington Gardens, London W2 3XA
T: *020 7298 1522* W: *www.serpentinegallery.org*

OPENING HOURS:
Open daily for private hire and events
Private Breakfast Views: 8:30am – 9:45am
Seated Dinners and Receptions: 6:30pm – 10:30pm

GOOD FOR HOSTING...
...a sparkling evening cocktail reception in a beautiful and impressive setting.
...a Champagne breakfast to impress guests.
...an elegant dinner and a private view of the current exhibition to entertain and excite prestigious guests.
...an extravaganza in the ***Serpentine Gallery Pavilion*** during the Summer months.
...a launch party or fashion show in stunning surroundings.

LOCATION: Kensington Gardens
NEAREST TUBE: South Kensington
FUNCTION ROOMS: 1
CAPACITY: 70 seated / 150 standing
PRIVATE DINING: N/A
CIVIL CEREMONIES: No
CUISINE: Flexible catering

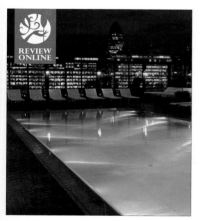

SHOREDITCH HOUSE
A PRIVATE MEMBERS' CLUB

"Members want for nothing at this uber cool club and the private hire spaces (available to all) are also some of the coolest around."

Ebor Street, London E1 6AW
T: *020 7749 4544* W: *www.shoreditchhouse.com*

OPENING HOURS:
Monday to Friday / Saturday / Sunday
8am – 3am / 10am – 3am / 10am – 10:30pm

GOOD FOR GOING OUT...
...if you're lucky enough to be a member.

GOOD FOR HOSTING...
...a fun bowling party in the private bar and bowling alley, ***Biscuit Pin***.
...a Christmas party with cocktails, canapés and dancing in the New York-style ***Biscuit Tin*** for a fun-loving crowd.
...a launch party for trendy-types in ***Biscuit Tin***.
...a pampering party for a group of girlfriends in ***Cowshed*** complete with treatments, Champagne and canapés.

LOCATION: Shoreditch
NEAREST TUBE: Shoreditch High St
FUNCTION ROOMS: 3
CAPACITY: 180 seated / 200 standing
PRIVATE DINING: 90, 180
CIVIL CEREMONIES: Yes
CUISINE: British

SHOREDITCH TOWN HALL
AN EVENT SPACE

"A unique space in an impressive building, Shoreditch Town Hall offers a break from the norm."

380 Old Street, London EC1V 9LT
T: *020 7739 6176* W: *www.shoreditchtownhall.org.uk*

OPENING HOURS:
Open daily for events and private hire

GOOD FOR HOSTING...
...a dramatic and large scale event with live entertainment and dancing in **The Assembly Hall**.
...a fashion show in **The Assembly Hall** for a quirky label.

LOCATION: Shoreditch
NEAREST TUBE: Old Street
FUNCTION ROOMS: 6
CAPACITY: 400 seated / 800 standing
PRIVATE DINING: N/A
CIVIL CEREMONIES: Yes
CUISINE: Flexible catering

SIMPSON'S-IN-THE-STRAND
A RESTAURANT

"Iconic and historic, this traditional venue remains a firm favourite."

100 Strand, London WC2R 0EW
T: *020 7836 9112* W: *www.simpsonsinthestrand.co.uk*

OPENING HOURS:
Monday to Friday
7:15am – 10:30am; 12:15pm – 2:45pm; 5:45pm – 10:45pm
Saturday / Sunday
12:15pm – 2:45pm / 3pm; 5:45pm / 6pm – 10:45pm / 9pm

GOOD FOR GOING OUT...
...for dinner in a grand but comfortable setting.
...for lunch if you're craving a roast to rival all roasts.
...for a man-sized breakfast to kick start the day.
...for a light, pre-theatre snack in the art deco **Knight's Bar** with your husband or wife.

GOOD FOR HOSTING...
...a roast lunch for your friends following a masterclass in the art of carving.
...a traditional banquet in a historic private event room.

LOCATION: The Strand
NEAREST TUBE: Charing Cross
FUNCTION ROOMS: 2
CAPACITY: 120 seated / 250 standing
PRIVATE DINING: 50, 120
CIVIL CEREMONIES: Yes
CUISINE: British

The Gallery

LOCATION: Mayfair
NEAREST TUBE: Oxford Circus
FUNCTION ROOMS: 5
CAPACITY: 150 seated / 650 standing
PRIVATE DINING: 24, 50, 50, 150
CIVIL CEREMONIES: Yes
CUISINE: Fusion / Modern European

SKETCH

A RESTAURANT & BAR

"With the Parlour's magical patisseries, the Gallery restaurant's panoramic video screens and the lavish Lecture Room, sketch tantalises all the senses."

---

9 Conduit Street, London W15 2XG
T: *020 7659 4500* W: *www.sketch.uk.com*

OPENING HOURS:
Monday to Saturday
8am – 2am

GOOD FOR GOING OUT...
...for afternoon tea with a group of girlfriends in **The Parlour**.
...for a lively dinner with friends to celebrate a birthday in the quirky **Gallery Room**.
...for Michelin-starred dining in the lavish **Lecture Room**.

GOOD FOR HOSTING...
...a quirky cocktail party for a fashionable crowd in **The Glade**, for up to 80 people.
...a dramatic launch party for up to 250 trendy-types in **The Gallery** and **East Bar**.
...an elegant dinner for 50 in the **Lecture Room** and **Library**.

LOCATION: The City
NEAREST TUBE: Tower Hill
FUNCTION ROOMS: 1
CAPACITY: 60 seated / 240 standing
PRIVATE DINING: 60
CIVIL CEREMONIES: Yes
CUISINE: British

SKYLOUNGE

A RESTAURANT & BAR

"Hidden up high, near The Tower of London, is SkyLounge: a bar and restaurant with stunning rooftop gardens with views across the city."

Mint Hotel, 7 Pepys Street, London EC3N 4AF
T: *020 7709 1000* W: *www.minthotel.com/our-hotels/london-tower-london/skylounge*

OPENING HOURS:
Open daily
10:30am – 2:00am

GOOD FOR GOING OUT...
...for drinks with a date, to impress them with the unexpected.
...for an informal but memorable client lunch.
...for dinner and drinks in a unique location with a group of friends looking to do something different.

GOOD FOR HOSTING...
...a unique and impressive alfresco party in stylish surroundings in the sky.
...a private dinner in a room with panoramic views, following reception drinks on the roof gardens outside.

THE SOHO HOTEL
A HOTEL

*"From the much-admired Firmdale group,
The Soho Hotel is as unique as it is chic."*

4 Richmond Mews, London W1D 3DH
T: *020 7559 3000* W: *www.firmdalehotels.com*

GOOD FOR GOING OUT...
...to the **Sunday Film Club** to enjoy a movie and either
afternoon tea or dinner in **Refuel**, for a relaxing end to the
weekend.

GOOD FOR HOSTING...
...an afternoon tea party with girlfriends in the **Library**.
...a cocktail party in **The Crimson Bar** to celebrate a launch.
...a candlelit dinner party with friends in **The Swirl Room**.
...a working lunch with stylish clients in the **Black and
White Room**.

LOCATION: Soho
NEAREST TUBE: Tottenham Court Rd
FUNCTION ROOMS: 6
CAPACITY: 70 seated / 300 standing
PRIVATE DINING: 10, 20, 50, 70
CIVIL CEREMONIES: Yes
CUISINE: British / Afternoon Tea

SOHO HOUSE
A PRIVATE MEMBERS' CLUB

*"Soho House is an institution; for work, pleasure
and parties, it has it nailed."*

21 Old Compton Street, London W1D 4EB
T: *020 7292 0122* W: *www.sohohouselondon.com*

OPENING HOURS:
Monday to Friday
8am – 3am
Saturday / Sunday
10am – 3am / 10:30pm

GOOD FOR GOING OUT...
...if you're lucky enough to be a member.

GOOD FOR HOSTING...
...a screening for up to 27 guests.
...a cocktail party with friends in the cosy but cool
House Basement, with a DJ and dancing.
...a fun client dinner in **Dining Room 19/21** for up to
42 people.
...a drinks party with a private bar in **Dining Room
19/21**, for up to 50 chic and trendy-types.

LOCATION: Soho
NEAREST TUBE: Tottenham Court Rd
FUNCTION ROOMS: 4
CAPACITY: 60 seated / 80 standing
PRIVATE DINING: 42
CIVIL CEREMONIES: Yes
CUISINE: British

SOMERSET HOUSE
AN EVENT SPACE

"For location and impressive impact, it doesn't get any better than Somerset House."

Strand, London WC2R 1LA
T: *0844 824 1698* W: *www.somersethouse.org.uk/events*

OPENING HOURS:
Open daily for events and private hire

GOOD FOR HOSTING...
...a neo-classical extravaganza in the *Fountain Court*.
...an exclusive alfresco drinks reception and sit down dinner on *The River Terrace* for wow factor.
...a launch party or exhibition in the contemporary and urban *Embankment East Room*.

LOCATION: The Strand
NEAREST TUBE: Charing Cross
FUNCTION ROOMS: 11
CAPACITY: 550 seated / 1,500 standing
PRIVATE DINING: 50, 80, 100, 250, 550
CIVIL CEREMONIES: Yes
CUISINE: Flexible catering

THE SQUARE
A RESTAURANT

"The Private Dining Room in this two Michelin-starred restaurant is as discreet as it gets."

6-10 Bruton Street, London W1J 6PU
T: *020 7495 7100* W: *www.squarerestaurant.com*

OPENING HOURS:
Monday to Friday
12pm – 2:30pm; 6:30pm – 10pm
Saturday / Sunday
6:30pm – 10:30pm / 9:30pm

GOOD FOR GOING OUT...
...for formal lunches with foodie enthusiasts.
...for an intimate and indulgent anniversary dinner with your husband or wife.

GOOD FOR HOSTING...
...an important client lunch or dinner where complete privacy is required, for 8 to 18 guests.
...a private dinner to mark a special occasion in smart but comfortable surroundings, with a focus on exceptional food and wine.

LOCATION: Mayfair
NEAREST TUBE: Green Park
FUNCTION ROOMS: 2
CAPACITY: 80 seated
PRIVATE DINING: 18, 80
CIVIL CEREMONIES: No
CUISINE: Modern European

ST JOHN BAR & RESTAURANT

A RESTAURANT & BAR

"It might not always sound irresistibly delicious, but this is an explorative, outstanding menu that will delight and astound again and again."

26 St John Street, London EC1M 4AY
T: 020 3301 8069 W: www.stjohnrestaurant.com

OPENING HOURS:
Monday to Friday
12pm – 3pm; 6pm – 11pm
Saturday
6pm – 11pm
Sunday
1pm – 4pm

GOOD FOR GOING OUT...
...with an adventurous food enthusiast.
...on a date for a quirky but delicious culinary experience in a relaxed and unique, unfussy setting.

GOOD FOR HOSTING...
...a feast with whole suckling pig for up to 16 friends to share and enjoy, in relaxed surroundings.

LOCATION: The City
NEAREST TUBE: Barbican
FUNCTION ROOMS: 2
CAPACITY: 110 seated / 130 standing
PRIVATE DINING: 18, 110
CIVIL CEREMONIES: No
CUISINE: Nose-to-Tail / British

ST MARTINS LANE

A HOTEL

"With Asia de Cuba, The Light Bar, Bungalow 8 and a plethora of event spaces, St Martins Lane has it all."

REVIEW ONLINE

Asia De Cuba

45 St Martins Lane, London WC2N 4HX
T: 020 7300 5500 W: www.stmartinslane.com

GOOD FOR GOING OUT...
...for intimate pre-dinner cocktails in **Light Bar** with a date.
...for a relaxed but sophisticated, hearty lunch with clients in **Asia de Cuba**.
...for a birthday dinner with a group of friends and family to enjoy delicious food and chic surroundings in **Asia de Cuba**.

GOOD FOR HOSTING...
...a sophisticated drinks party for stylish guests, in the unique white marble **Back Room**, complete with a small, private outdoor terrace.
...a private and intimate dinner and drinks reception in the **Penthouse suite**.

LOCATION: West End
NEAREST TUBE: Leicester Square
FUNCTION ROOMS: 3
CAPACITY: 96 seated / 180 standing
PRIVATE DINING: 48, 96
CIVIL CEREMONIES: Yes
CUISINE: Asian-Latino

STAFFORD LONDON BY KEMPINSKI

A HOTEL

"Where tradition meets modernity in a calm and elegant setting off St James's."

The American Bar

St James's Place, London SW1A 1NJ
T: *020 7493 0111* W: *www.kempinski.com/london*

OPENING HOURS:

Monday to Saturday / Sunday
Bar: 11:30am – 11pm / 12pm – 11pm
Restaurant: 7am – 11am; 12pm – 2:30pm; 6pm – 10:30pm / 8am – 9:30pm

GOOD FOR GOING OUT...

...for a low-key lunch with clients in the atmospheric ***American Bar*** that's relaxed and filled with character.

...for after work drinks in ***The American Bar*** with clients.

...for dinner in ***The Lyttelton***, the newly opened restaurant.

GOOD FOR HOSTING...

...a private dinner with a wine tasting in the vaulted wine cellar.

...an elegant wedding in traditionally British surroundings.

LOCATION: Mayfair
NEAREST TUBE: Green Park
FUNCTION ROOMS: 5
CAPACITY: 44 seated / 75 standing
PRIVATE DINING: 8, 12, 38, 44
CIVIL CEREMONIES: Yes
CUISINE: British

THE SUMMERHOUSE

A RESTAURANT

"The Summerhouse is a place to go when you need to get respite from London and your hectic life."

60 Blomfield Road, London W9 2PD
T: *020 7286 6752* W: *www.summerhousebythewaterway.co.uk*

OPENING HOURS:

Monday to Friday
12pm – 11pm
Saturday / Sunday
10am – 11pm / 10am – 10:30pm

GOOD FOR GOING OUT...

...for a lunch with friends, during April to November, to feel like you are on holiday.

...for river views and an alfresco setting.

...for a date on a Summer evening to enjoy a bottle of rosé and British fare in relaxed surroundings.

GOOD FOR HOSTING...

...an atmospheric drinks party in a unique riverside, alfresco-style setting during Winter months.

LOCATION: Maida Vale
NEAREST TUBE: Warwick Avenue
FUNCTION ROOMS: 1
CAPACITY: 50 seated / 70 standing
PRIVATE DINING: 50
CIVIL CEREMONIES: No
CUISINE: British

SUMOSAN
A RESTAURANT

"It might not be as shouted-about as other Japanese restaurants, but that's because those in-the-know want to keep it a secret. Expensive but exceptional sushi."

26 Albemarle Street, London W1S 4HY
T: 020 7495 5999 W: www.sumosan.com

OPENING HOURS:
Monday to Friday
12pm – 2:45pm; 6pm – 11:30pm
Saturday / Sunday
6pm – 11:30pm / 6pm – 10:30pm

GOOD FOR GOING OUT...
...for a formal lunch with clients in a chic setting.
...for a dinner date with a glamorous sushi lover.
...for relaxed but sophisticated after-work drinks and plates of sushi in the *J Bar*, with colleagues and friends.

GOOD FOR HOSTING...
...a drinks and canapés party or sake tasting for clients in the relaxed, comfortable and stylish *J Bar*.

LOCATION: Mayfair
NEAREST TUBE: Green Park
FUNCTION ROOMS: 2
CAPACITY: 120 seated / 200 standing
PRIVATE HIRE: 32, 120
CIVIL CEREMONIES: No
CUISINE: Japanese

SUPPERCLUB
A RESTAURANT & NIGHTCLUB

"With no airs and graces, supperclub has a wonderful disarming atmosphere that provokes relaxation and profligacy, camaraderie as well as naughtiness."

12 Acklam Road, London W10 5QZ
T: 020 8964 6600 W: www.supperclub.com

OPENING HOURS:
Monday to Saturday / Sunday
6pm – 2am / 11am – 6pm

GOOD FOR GOING OUT... ·
...for late night dancing with trendy and edgy friends.
...with a large group of friends for a unique dining experience whilst you lounge on beds and watch live entertainment, before dancing the night away.
...for a hedonistic weekend brunch on selected dates.

GOOD FOR HOSTING...
...a launch party or fashion show in the large and urban white-washed main space, for a trendy and fashion-focused crowd.
...private parties in the tucked away VIP room.

LOCATION: Notting Hill
NEAREST TUBE: Ladbroke Grove
FUNCTION ROOMS: 1
CAPACITY: 155 seated / 500 standing
PRIVATE DINING: 155
CIVIL CEREMONIES: Yes
CUISINE: Modern European

LOCATION: Mayfair
NEAREST TUBE: Green Park
FUNCTION ROOMS: 1
CAPACITY: 84 seated
PRIVATE DINING: 84
CIVIL CEREMONIES: No
CUISINE: Indian

TAMARIND
A RESTAURANT

"Exquisite Indian cuisine in a fine-dining atmosphere makes Tamarind a popular choice with the Mayfair set."

20 Queen Street, London W1J 5PR
T: *020 7629 3561* W: *www.tamarindrestaurant.com*

OPENING HOURS:
Monday to Saturday / Sunday
12pm – 2:45pm (closed Saturday lunch); 5:30pm – 11pm /
12pm – 2:45pm; 6pm – 10:30pm

GOOD FOR GOING OUT...
…for lunch with clients who you want to impress with
    stunning food, great wine and impeccable service.
…for an intimate and lavish dinner with a lover of
    authentic Indian haute cuisine.
…for lunch or dinner in a luxurious but refined setting
    in central Mayfair for a group of up to 20 people.

GOOD FOR HOSTING...
…a high-end Indian banquet in any location of your
    choice, with Tamarind's Event Catering service.

LOCATION: Belgravia
NEAREST TUBE: Victoria
FUNCTION ROOMS: 4
CAPACITY: 42 seated / 120 standing
PRIVATE DINING: 12, 20, 30, 42
CIVIL CEREMONIES: No
CUISINE: British

THE THOMAS CUBITT
A PUBLIC HOUSE

"The Thomas Cubitt is a charming, atmospheric pub that pulls a local, sociable crowd."

44 Elizabeth Street, London SW1W 9PA
T: *020 7730 6060* W: *www.thethomascubitt.co.uk*

OPENING HOURS:
Monday to Saturday / Sunday
12pm – 11pm / 12pm – 10:30pm

GOOD FOR GOING OUT...
…on a relaxed date in a cosy, classic country pub-style
    setting, on the ground floor (no reservations).
…for a low-key catch up with friends.
…for an intimate date in the chic first floor dining room.
…for a low-key birthday dinner with your family.

GOOD FOR HOSTING...
…a relaxed drinks party for up to 20 close friends in
    The Atrium with an open fire place.
…an informal but refined working lunch for up to 12 clients.

TOM'S KITCHEN

A RESTAURANT

"Tom's Kitchen has a chic but informal atmosphere all day long; a favourite with the Chelsea locals."

27 Cale Street, London SW3 3QP
T: *020 7349 0202* W: *www.tomskitchen.co.uk/chelsea*

OPENING HOURS:
Monday to Friday / Saturday and Sunday
8am – 11am; 12pm – 3pm; 6pm – 11pm /
10am – 4pm; 6pm – 11pm

GOOD FOR GOING OUT...
...for a leisurely weekend brunch with friends and the papers, in the **Brasserie**.
...for a low-key birthday lunch with friends on the first floor.
...for a relaxed dinner date in informal and rustic surroundings, in the **Brasserie**.
...for pre-dinner drinks in the first floor bar.

GOOD FOR HOSTING...
...a relaxed but sophisticated dinner in a comfortable townhouse-style private dining room, following reception drinks in a private lounge area.

LOCATION: Chelsea
NEAREST TUBE: South Kensington
FUNCTION ROOMS: 2
CAPACITY: 40 seated / 75 standing
PRIVATE DINING: 22, 40
CIVIL CEREMONIES: No
CUISINE: British

TRAMP

A PRIVATE MEMBERS' CLUB

"Tramp combines glamour, historical charm and a gentleman's club air, with a vibrant crowd who know how to party."

40 Jermyn Street, London SW1Y 6DN
T: *020 7734 0565* W: *www.tramp.co.uk*

OPENING HOURS:
Friday and Saturday
8pm – late

GOOD FOR GOING OUT...
...if you're lucky enough to be a member.
...with a member for a night of dancing and decadence to witness the new and impressive smoking terrace and lounge bar, opening in June 2011.

GOOD FOR HOSTING...
...a unique and sophisticated private dinner or drinks party in a space that combines tradition with contemporary glamour.

LOCATION: Mayfair
NEAREST TUBE: Piccadilly Circus
FUNCTION ROOMS: 2
CAPACITY: 80 seated / 200 standing
PRIVATE DINING: 80
CIVIL CEREMONIES: No
CUISINE: Modern European

LOCATION: South Kensington
NEAREST TUBE: South Kensington
FUNCTION ROOMS: 3
CAPACITY: 400 seated / 600 standing
PRIVATE DINING: 230, 400
CIVIL CEREMONIES: No
CUISINE: Flexible catering

THE V&A
AN EVENT SPACE

"This beautiful Victorian building houses a myriad of event spaces, as well as its impressive art collections."

Cromwell Road, London SW7 2RL
T: *020 7942 2646 / 2647* W: *www.vam.ac.uk*

OPENING HOURS:
Open daily for events and private hire

GOOD FOR HOSTING...
...a Summer wedding reception with wow factor in
  The John Madejski Garden.
...a corporate dinner-dance in the unique and memorable
  Dome entrance.
...an atmospheric and dramatic dinner with speeches
  and presentations in the impressive and prestigious
  Raphael Gallery.

LOCATION: Trafalgar Square
NEAREST TUBE: Charing Cross
FUNCTION ROOMS: 5
CAPACITY: 420 seated / 520 standing
PRIVATE DINING: 18, 24, 48, 150, 180
CIVIL CEREMONIES: Yes
CUISINE: Modern European

VISTA
A BAR

"A stylish oasis above the chaos of Trafalgar Square, Vista is a hidden gem with a chic Mediterranean vibe."

The Trafalgar, 2 Spring Gardens, London SW1A 2TS
T: *020 7870 2900* W: *www.vistaatthetrafalgar.co.uk*

OPENING HOURS:
Monday – Saturday / Sunday
12pm – 1am / 11pm

GOOD FOR GOING OUT...
...for after-work drinks to unwind on the stylish rooftop.
...on a date to admire the view and get cosy under blankets
  when the sun goes down.
...to impress an out-of-towner in a relaxed but chic setting.
GOOD FOR HOSTING...
...a stylish, alfresco Summer drinks party with a live grill,
  to discreetly impress guests.
...an outdoor, late-night screening.

WHISKY MIST
A NIGHTCLUB

"Whisky Mist pulls a jetset crowd with many an A-lister joining in with the fun."

35 Hertford Street, London W1J 7SD
T: *020 7208 4067* W: *www.whiskymist.com*

OPENING HOURS:
Tuesday to Sunday
10:30pm – 3am

GOOD FOR GOING OUT...
...on a Sunday night for their biggest night, with a beautiful friend who does not need to work the next day.
...any night of the week (except for a Monday) for cocktails and dancing amidst a wealthy crowd.

GOOD FOR HOSTING...
...a hedonistic Christmas party on a Monday night, for a party-keen crowd.
...an early evening product launch in a sexy and seductive space.
...an exclusive after party for VIPs.

LOCATION: Mayfair
NEAREST TUBE: Hyde Park Corner
FUNCTION ROOMS: 2
CAPACITY: 240 standing
PRIVATE DINING: N/A
CIVIL CEREMONIES: No
CUISINE: N/A

THE WOLSELEY
A RESTAURANT

"Regardless of the time of day, The Wolseley is an absolute winner for those seeking laid-back glamour."

160 Piccadilly, London W1J 9EB
T: *020 7499 6996* W: *www.thewolseley.com*

OPENING HOURS:
Monday to Friday
7am – 12am
Saturday
8am – 12am
Sunday
8am – 11pm

GOOD FOR GOING OUT...
...for breakfast and brunch with someone stylish and refined.
...for lunch with clients in a buzzy but sophisticated setting to enjoy British cuisine amongst a glamorous Mayfair set.
...for a date with someone sociable and chic.
...for pre-theatre dinner with your parents.

LOCATION: Mayfair
NEAREST TUBE: Green Park
FUNCTION ROOMS: 1
CAPACITY: 12 seated
PRIVATE DINING: 12
CIVIL CEREMONIES: No
CUISINE: European

ZAFFERANO

A RESTAURANT

"This Michelin-starred Italian is a destination restaurant as well as a hit with the locals."

15 Lowndes Street, London SW1X 9EY
T: *020 7235 5800* W: *www.atozrestaurants.com/zafferano*

OPENING HOURS:

Monday to Friday
12pm – 2:30pm; 7pm – 11pm
Saturday and Sunday
12:30pm – 3pm; 7pm – 10:30pm

GOOD FOR GOING OUT...
...with a lover of fine Italian cuisine.
...for a relaxed but formal lunch or dinner with clients.
...for lunch with a glamorous girlfriend.
...for an intimate and low-key anniversary dinner with your
   husband or wife.

GOOD FOR HOSTING...
...an atmospheric birthday dinner with friends and family,
   in the unique private dining room, complete with exposed
   brick, a vaulted ceiling and views of the wine cellar.

LOCATION: Knightsbridge
NEAREST TUBE: Knightsbridge
FUNCTION ROOMS: 1
CAPACITY: 20 seated
PRIVATE DINING: 20
CIVIL CEREMONIES: No
CUISINE: Italian

ZUMA

A RESTAURANT & BAR

"Informal but stylish, Zuma pulls the monied-set thanks to great food and a fantastic atmosphere, every night of the week."

5 Raphael Street, London SW7 1DL
T: *020 7584 1010* W: *www.zumarestaurant.com*

OPENING HOURS:

Monday to Friday
12pm – 3pm; 6pm – 11pm
Saturday / Sunday
12:30pm – 3:30pm; 6pm – 11pm / 6pm – 10:30pm

GOOD FOR GOING OUT...
...for drinks and dinner with someone glamorous and sociable.
...for after-work drinks in elegant and buzzy surroundings.
...with clients for an indulgent lunch.

GOOD FOR HOSTING...
...a dinner to celebrate your birthday for up to 14 friends
   in the semi-private dining room.
...a semi-private lunch for fun-loving clients.
...a celebratory dinner following drinks in the bar.

LOCATION: Knightsbridge
NEAREST TUBE: Knightsbridge
FUNCTION ROOMS: 2
CAPACITY: 14 seated
PRIVATE DINING: 12, 14
CIVIL CEREMONIES: No
CUISINE: Japanese

GALLERY OF SERVICES

SNOOK EVENTS

ORGANISING, PLANNING & PRODUCTION

The perfect party or event runs seamlessly and looks effortless, but – like the proverbial swan – a polished result takes a fair amount of work.

Listed here are the best in the business at planning and delivering the most spectacular parties and events in London, the UK and beyond.

ADMIRABLE CRICHTON
A PARTY ORGANISER

"If parties were measured by hammers and bells, The AC would smash the bell off the top every time."

T: *020 7326 3800* W: *www.admirable-crichton.co.uk*

GOOD FOR...
...a bespoke wedding or party with stunning, creative design and live entertainment, anywhere in the world.
...innovative culinary expertise with Royal Warrant approval.

APOLLO EVENT CONSULTANTS
A PARTY ORGANISER

"Consistently exceeding expectations by producing impeccably executed, highly creative, original events."

T: *0845 883 3403* W: *www.apollo-ec.co.uk*

GOOD FOR...
...a milestone birthday party with flair and charm.
...a countryside wedding in a dramatically adorned marquee.
...bespoke hospitality at any global sporting occasion.

AT YOUR SERVICE
AN EVENT STAFFING COMPANY

"Supplying experienced, reliable staff to events, At Your Service is aptly named."

T: *020 7610 8610* W: *www.ays.co.uk*

GOOD FOR...

...articulate, attractive and highly trained bar and waiting staff.
...bespoke uniforms for all staff roles and themes.
...baristas, sommeliers, kitchen porters and specialist staff.

AURA
A STRATEGIC EVENT PLANNER

"Creative and strategic events for corporate clients, with a primary focus on building business relations."

T: *020 7963 0680* W: *www.auralimited.co.uk*

GOOD FOR...

...an international conference that breaks the expected mould.
...a launch party or bespoke event with key brand messages.
...a private dinner with exacting standards for VIPs.

THE BANK EVENTS
A PARTY ORGANISER

"The Bank creates, strategically plans, produces and delivers all manner of high impact live events."

T: *020 7612 8000* W: *www.thebank.co.uk*

GOOD FOR...

...event production (including stage design, lighting, filming, graphics and more) for some of the world's top events, from small scale conferences to large outdoor launch events.

BENTLEY'S ENTERTAINMENTS
A PARTY ORGANISER

"With many celebrity clients, Bentley's knows a thing or two about wow factor."

T: *020 7223 7900* W: *www.bentleys.net*

GOOD FOR...

...a mind-blowing wedding in a lavish location.
...an intimate, stylish and delicately detailed private party.
...a creative, memorable and jaw-dropping event for VIPs.

BEYOND
A STRATEGIC EVENT PLANNER

"Combine commercial acumen with creative flair to take you further."

T: *020 7289 3000* W: *www.beyondevents.co.uk*

GOOD FOR...

...bespoke client and staff entertaining.

...events that are integral to your communication strategy.

...going BEYOND: how far do you want to go?

CRAFTY ARTY PARTIES
A CHILDREN'S PARTY ORGANISER

"From entertainers and party bags to adventures and Hogwarts-style banquets, Crafty Arty Parties are specialists in exceptional children's events."

T: *020 7060 2320* W: *www.craftyartyparties.com*

GOOD FOR...

...a family fun day with world-class entertainers and games.

...a launch for a child-focused brand.

EVENTORACLE
A PARTY ORGANISER & CATERER

"EventOracle's young team (wise beyond their years) keep events fresh, fun and creative."

T: *020 8961 7477* W: *www.eventoracle.com*

GOOD FOR...

...a themed birthday party, stacked with creative ideas.

...a classic and beautiful country-style wedding.

...a spectacular event for any budget.

HALO LIGHTING
A LIGHTING & PRODUCTION COMPANY

"The most advanced, but accessible, lighting and special effects for parties and events."

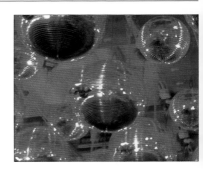

T: *0844 844 0484* W: *www.halo.co.uk*

GOOD FOR...

...house parties to large-scale events.

...impressive lighting and unrivalled special effects including LEDs, lasers, confetti cannons, pyrotechnics and more.

HIGH SOCIETY
AN EVENT STAFFING COMPANY

"First impressions are everything; let High Society ensure you make the right one."

T: *020 7228 0333* W: *www.high-society.co.uk*

GOOD FOR...

...articulate, hardworking, efficient staff, including baristas, cocktail waiters and fine-dining waitstaff, for all occasions.

...last minute staffing needs.

KASIMIRA
A PARTY ORGANISER

"Enjoy exceptional results with a focus on unique and personal touches, regardless of scale or location."

T: *020 7581 8313* W: *www.kasimira.com*

GOOD FOR...

...an exquisite wedding full of charm and creativity.

...an imaginative and fun private party with wow factor.

...a luxurious, event-packed, weekend getaway.

LAST SUPPER
A PARTY ORGANISER & CATERER

"With great food and exemplary staff, an event catered by Last Supper will be picture perfect."

T: *020 7378 0101* W: *www.lastsupperltd.co.uk*

GOOD FOR...

...good looking, charming and intelligent waiting staff.

...a unique and quirky event, infused with atmosphere through style, design, food, drinks and aromas.

LES ENFANTS
A CHILDREN'S PARTY ORGANISER

"Les Enfants offer a full range of services, from birthday parties to crèches to large corporate events."

T: *020 8502 9988* W: *www.lesenfants.co.uk*

GOOD FOR...

...launch parties and premieres for child-focused products.

...rewarding and valuable corporate family fun days.

...a fun wedding crèche to keep the little ones at bay.

LINDA COOPER WEDDINGS
A WEDDING PLANNER

"Ultimate perfection as delivered by Linda Cooper comes at a price, but it will be worth it."

T: 020 7624 0822 W: *www.lindacooperweddings.com*

GOOD FOR...

...a big-budget, unique and distinctive wedding or civil
 partnership with flair and finesse.

...a luxury wedding in the Caribbean, Europe and USA.

MELON
A PARTY ORGANISER

"Adopting a creative and strategic approach to planning perfect private and corporate events."

T: 020 3405 1946 W: *www.melonevents.co.uk*

GOOD FOR...

...an extravagant and indulgent car park picnic.

...a picnic in the park with games for a fun Summer party.

...a bespoke Summer or Christmas party package from MELON.

NIEMIERKO
A WEDDING PLANNER

"Niemierko excels at planning weddings and events for the savviest of clients, all over the world."

T: 020 7580 5010 W: *www.niemierko.com*

GOOD FOR...

...an extravagant wedding reflective of your personal style.

...an intimate and sublimely stylish London civil partnership.

...any event that requires a perfect blend of luxury and taste.

OPM
A PARTY ORGANISER

"OPM plan imaginative parties packed with character, all across the globe."

T: 020 7731 1008 W: *www.opmpartnership.com*

GOOD FOR...

...an elegant, discreet and immaculately planned party.

...an impressive corporate event that feels private.

...a truly fabulous wedding.

PARTRIDGE EVENTS
AN EVENT PRODUCTION COMPANY

"For creative event production and party design, if you're game, so are Partridge."

T: *0845 308 2427* W: *www.partridgeevents.co.uk*

GOOD FOR...

...any party requiring the creative eye of a designer to transform a space into something spectacular.

...a launch party reflective of the brand's image and ethos.

PAUL SIMON EVENTS
A PARTY ORGANISER

"PS Events is a boutique company, offering a personable and dynamic service."

T: *07917 453755* W: *www.paulsimonevents.co.uk*

GOOD FOR...

...a fun day or incentive trip, focusing on developing relationships amongst colleagues and clients.

...corporate dinners, events or occasions to meet all budgets.

PROP DEAD GORGEOUS
A FURNITURE & PROP HIRE COMPANY

"Collaborated by a team of experts who have been theming and dressing spectacular parties around the world for over decade."

T: *1300 345 397* W: *www.propdeadgorgeous.com*

GOOD FOR...

...an array of unique props and styling expertise to give your party wow factor.

QUINTESSENTIALLY EVENTS
A PARTY ORGANISER

"Part of the luxury lifestyle group, Quintessentially Events sure do know how to throw a party."

T: *0845 4758 400* W: *www.quintessentiallyevents.com*

GOOD FOR...

...a star-studded and luxurious, extravagant event.

...a decadent private party anywhere in the world.

...a once in a lifetime adventure, laced with luxury.

RED CARPET SECURITY
AN EVENT STAFFING COMPANY

"Red carpet Security offers an experienced team of specialists to ensure VIP events run smoothly."

T: 020 7060 4321 W: *www.redcarpetsecurity.co.uk*

GOOD FOR...
...reliable, well-presented and highly-trained event security.
...valet parking to go that extra mile for your guests (literally).
...efficient and reliable crew for events.

ROUGE EVENTS
A STRATEGIC EVENT PLANNER

"Integrating creative events into corporate marketing and communication strategies."

T: *020 7514 5854* W: *www.rouge-events.com*

GOOD FOR...
...an imaginative and spectacular private party.
...an exciting launch or brand communication event.
...innovative festivals and live experiences.

SHARKY & GEORGE
A CHILDREN'S PARTY ORGANISER

"Sharky and George specialise in children's parties injecting energy and fun into everything they do."

T: *020 7924 4381* W: *www.sharkyandgeorge.com*

GOOD FOR...
...a kid's mini-disco with dancing, competitions and games.
...a treasure hunt, a cooking party, or an outdoor adventure.
...a children's party that's fun for everyone – even the parents.

SNOOK EVENTS
A PARTY ORGANISER

"No task is too large and no element is too small; Snook's attention to detail is exceptional."

T: *020 7692 5100* W: *www.snookevents.co.uk*

GOOD FOR...
...a creatively themed private party with wow factor.
...a seamless and classic, fairytale wedding.
...any event that involves meticulous planning.

TABLE TALK
A PARTY ORGANISER & CATERER

"Offering beautifully designed, sensational food, your party will be the talk of the town with Table Talk."

T: *020 7401 3200* W: *www.tabletalk.co.uk*

GOOD FOR...

...canapés as beautifully designed as the surroundings.
...sensational and sophisticated events on any scale.
...a luxurious and indulgent dinner at home.

THEME TRADERS
A PARTY ORGANISER & PROP HIRE COMPANY

"As well as organising showstopping parties, Theme Traders has incredible props for hire."

T: *020 8452 8518* W: *www.themetraders.com*

GOOD FOR...

...an extravagant party or event with elaborate room
  dressing, design, theming and impressive props.
...a milestone birthday with entertainment and wow factor.

TIKES & TIARAS
A CHILDREN'S PARTY ORGANISER

"Diamond encrusted party invitations? Dress-up in couture costumes? They're not kidding."

T: *020 7060 2320* W: *www.tikesandtiaras.com*

GOOD FOR...

...a bespoke and lavish party for a very discerning youngster.
...a jaw-dropping Bar or Bat Mitzvah to amaze and entertain
  guests of all ages.

TWIZZLE
A CHILDREN'S PARTY ORGANISER

"With over 25 years experience, Twizzle will show you a way to twizzle them around your little finger."

T: *020 8392 0860* W: *www.twizzle.co.uk*

GOOD FOR...

...a magical and stress-free party to suit all budgets.
...a stylish and memorable Bar or Bat Mitzvah.
...a family fun day with rides and amusement arcades.

URBAN CAPRICE
A PARTY ORGANISER

"As part of the Caprice restaurant group, you know you will get exquisite service every step of the way."

T: *020 7286 1700* W: *www.urbancaprice.co.uk*

GOOD FOR...

...imaginative and effective event styling and design.

...bringing the renowned food of The Ivy, Le Caprice and
  Scott's to your home or event, regardless of scale or location.

CATERERS

FOOD DELIVERY SERVICE

MAILABLE TREATS

FOOD & DRINK

Whether you're entertaining at home or out the back of your car, planning a wedding banquet, canapé party or corporate feast, every mouthful matters.

Listed here are London's top caterers, between them seeing to your every catering need with flair, finesse and zeal.

ARCHIE'S AT HOME
A CATERER

"For dinner parties, picnics, parties and weddings, Archie's delivers a personal, exquisite service."

T: *07867 525 371* W: *www.archiesathome.com*

GOOD FOR...

...a relaxed, hassle-free, exceptional dinner party at home.

...a seamless gourmet car park picnic service.

...an impeccable and discreet canapé party for VIPs.

AT HOME CATERING
A CATERER

"At Home will make you feel so relaxed you will feel, well, at home."

T: *01932 862 026* W: *www.athomecatering.co.uk*

GOOD FOR...

...transforming your home into a party paradise.

...imaginative, beautifully presented food and drink.

...a dynamic corporate event to suit all budgets.

BERRY SCRUMPTIOUS
A MAILABLE TREATS COMPANY

"Send chocolate dipped strawberries (fresh and decorated) to make somebody love you forever."

T: *01346 571 111* W: *www.berryscrumptious.co.uk*

GOOD FOR...

...congratulating a bride-to-be or a new mum by sending beautifully decorated strawberries.

...chocolate-dipped strawberry canapés at any event.

BLUE STRAWBERRY
A CATERER

"The name of this company is testament to their creativity and ability to think outside of the punnet."

T: *020 7326 5742* W: *www.bluestrawberry.co.uk*

GOOD FOR HOSTING...

...a creative and delectable wedding banquet.

...a sensational and sophisticated event on any scale.

...an environmentally-friendly wedding day.

CALLY B
A CATERER

"Providing a first-class, flexible and friendly service for 25 years...with Cally B, you are in safe hands."

T: *020 7610 2266* W: *www.callyb.co.uk*

GOOD FOR...

...consistently outstanding catering for all occasions.

...combining the latest trends with the finest ingredients.

...providing a discreet, reputable and reliable service.

DELIVERANCE
A FOOD DELIVERY COMPANY

"Gourmet, multi-cuisine food delivery service on a mission to change London takeaway."

T: *0844 875 0400* W: *www.deliverance.co.uk*

GOOD FOR...

...hot, fresh, restaurant-quality food, prepared and delivered to enjoy in the comfort of your own home.

...takeaway with a difference, whatever cuisine you fancy.

DE WINTONS
A CATERER

"deWintons deliver innovative food for both private and corporate markets, with passion."

T: *020 7627 5550* W: *www.dewintons.co.uk*

GOOD FOR...

...canapés that reflect any theme and satisfy all appetites.
...bespoke and exceptional menus (for picnics and tea parties, weddings and events), to suit all budgets and scales.

DOUGHDOUGH.COM
A MAILABLE TREATS COMPANY

"Whatever the sentiment, say it with edible, mailable, affordable treats."

T: *01480 225 665* W: *www.doughdough.com*

GOOD FOR...

...making someone smile with a card and a brownie for under £5.
...an invitation to a party, to get guests excited from the off.
...a fun way to communicate with clients.

MODEL CATERING
A CATERER & EVENT STAFF PROVIDER

"A model example of how food should be prepared, cooked, presented and served."

T: *020 8964 1712* W: *www.modelcatering.com*

GOOD FOR...

...beautiful food served by beautiful people.
...exciting food whether you're catering for 2, 20 or 200.
...a designer diet delivered daily to your door.

NOBLE HOUSE EVENTS
A CATERER

"Combining experience with a modern touch, Noble House Events is a wonderful addition to any event."

T: *020 7617 7477* W: *www.noblehouseevents.com*

GOOD FOR...

...a stunning canapé and cocktail reception or magnificent dinner, whatever the venue.
...catering that adds style and ambiance to any occasion.

PICNIC2U
A FOOD DELIVERY COMPANY

"No fuss, no mess, no compromise – Picnic2U offer wonderfully fresh picnics in throw-away boxes."

T: 020 8961 7477 W: *www.picnic2u.co.uk*

GOOD FOR...

...hand-prepared, ready-to-go picnics delivered to you,
  for enjoyment with friends or for any occasion.
...a bespoke, luxury picnic for a special event or date.

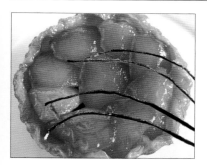

ROCKET FOOD
A CATERER

"A boutique catering company with creative flair, Rocket is the name on everyone's lips."

T: 020 7622 2320 W: *www.rocketfood.net*

GOOD FOR...

...ingredients sourced from small, artisan producers.
...food with distinctive character, served by charming staff.
...private parties and large scale events at prestigious venues.

TRUE DELI
A CATERER

"True Deli offers a personable service, delivering top quality dishes for both large and small events."

T: 020 7193 3275 W: *www.truedeli.co.uk*

GOOD FOR...

...great value, stunning canapé parties and wedding banquets.
...a bespoke delivery service for all forms of at home dining.
...hampers brimming with top-quality artisan produce.

ZAFFERANO
A CATERER

"Zafferano consistently maintains a personal approach to savvy party planning and catering."

T: 020 8905 9120 W: *www.zafferano.co.uk*

GOOD FOR...

...beautiful canapés at a stylish event of any size.
...an inspired menu at a flamboyant wedding.
...traditional catering in some of London's most iconic venues.

THE BEST IN ENTERTAINMENT

It's not just children that require entertainment; everyone likes a bit of a spectacle to hold their attention and capture their imagination.

From music and magicians, to interactive experiences and once in a lifetime adventures, these companies leave no stone unturned to ensure your event stands out from the crowd.

COOKIE CRUMBLES
CHILDREN'S PARTY ENTERTAINMENT

"Sometimes children's parties look more fun than adults' ones; that's just the way the cookie crumbles."

T: *020 8876 9912* W: *www.cookiecrumbles.co.uk*

GOOD FOR...
...a fun and educational cooking party for children in the
   comfort of your own home.
...a cooking party on any scale for children aged 4 to 18.

GENIE FILM
A FILM PRODUCTION COMPANY

"The only company on the planet specialising in sky-is-the-limit cinema films for private individuals."

T: *020 7121 6350* W: *www.geniefilm.com*

GOOD FOR...
...luxury, bespoke film-making for private clients.
...commemorating a special occasion with a cinema-style film.
...the ultimate gift for someone who has everything.

IBIZA ANGELS
PAMPERING AT EVENTS

"Offering on-site massage, combining relaxation with hedonistic party culture."

T: *0844 800 0013* W: *www.ibizaangels.com*

GOOD FOR...
...indulging guests with an invigorating 7 minute massage.
...engaging guests through the medium of massage.
...articulate, well presented staff to complement your event.

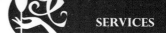

KEITH PROWSE
A HOSPITALITY PROVIDER

"Sporting or social, with friends or with clients, Keith Prowse can get you there."

T: *0845 415 0626* W: *www.keithprowse.co.uk*

GOOD FOR...

...leading hospitality at key sporting occasions across the globe.

...hassle-free and affordable days out with clients, colleagues, friends and families at Lords and Twickenham.

MOVIE PARTIES
A FILM PRODUCTION COMPANY

"Your special day. Your home. Your friends. Your very own film premiere."

T: *020 7121 6352* W: *www.movie-parties.co.uk*

GOOD FOR...

...parties for adults and parties for kids.

...celebrating a special day, by starring in your own film.

...filming it and screening it in one fun, action-packed day.

MYSTICAL FAIRIES
CHILDREN'S PARTY ENTERTAINMENT

"Fairytales aren't just restricted to bedtime; they're real and your little one can be the star."

T: *020 7431 1888* W: *www.mysticalfairies.co.uk*

GOOD FOR...

...a magical party in the **Enchanted Garden** in Hampstead, filled with fairies, princesses and all things glittery.

...a party anywhere with fairies, princesses, tea parties and more.

NOTORIOUS PRODUCTIONS
A PARTY ORGANISER & ENTERTAINMENT PROVIDER

"Bespoke entertainment experiences, first dance choreography, children's parties: Notorious do it all."

T: *020 8682 2799* W: *www.notoriousproductions.co.uk*

GOOD FOR...

...performers and themed experiences for events.

...first dance choreography to impress guests.

...parties for kids including pop star recording parties.

THE POWDERPUFF GIRLS
PAMPERING AT EVENTS

"Indulge your guests with luxurious primping and preening, courtesy of the fabulous Powderpuff Girls."

T: *0844 879 4928* W: *www.thepowderpuffgirls.com*

GOOD FOR...

...adding glamour to any event with The Powderpuff Girls dressed immaculately in 1950's style outfits.

...pampering guests with makeup, manicures and hairstyling.

SODEXO PRESTIGE
A HOSPITALITY PROVIDER

RHS Chelsea Flower Show

"With a focus on fabulous food, Sodexo offers corporate hospitality at leading sporting and social events."

T: *020 8831 3946* W: *www.sodexoprestige.co.uk*

GOOD FOR...

...a day to remember with golf enthusiasts at The Open.

...a VIP experience at Royal Ascot or Henley Royal Regatta.

...a fun day out with clients at RHS Chelsea Flower Show.

VITALI MUSIC
AN ENTERTAINMENT PROVIDER

"Offering the complete spectrum of live music genres, whatever your musical tastes Vitali can provide it."

T: *020 7127 4115* W: *www.vitalimusic.com*

GOOD FOR...

...any party or event requiring top quality live music, from symphonies to steel bands, classical singers to cabaret routines, tribute acts to tango medleys.

YOUNG GUNS
AN ENTERTAINMENT PROVIDER

"Young Guns is a cutting-edge music management company offering leading entertainment for events."

T: *020 7495 6606* W: *www.younggunsuk.com*

GOOD FOR...

...wowing guests with internationally acclaimed acts including the beautiful Escala and opera singing quartet, Passionata.

...live entertainers from DJs to orchestras, singers to dancers.

FINISHING TOUCHES

Exquisite 'finishing touches' are what cause eyes to pop and jaws to drop; they're what turn a good party into a fabulous one, a client event into a relationship builder.

From exceptional invites and beautiful flowers to the perfect gifts, these companies are the best at what they do.

SPECIALIST STATIONERS

FLORISTS

GIFTING

CALLIGRAPHY

BIRKSEN
A FLORIST

"A personable service, catering for all your flower needs, from styling weddings to magazine shoots."

T: *020 7622 6466* W: *www.birksen.co.uk*

GOOD FOR...
...classic wedding arrangements.
...modern and creative floral displays.
...table dressing and floral gifts at intimate parties.

FORTNUM & MASON
A GIFTING COMPANY

"Synonymous with luxury and quintessentially British, Fortnum's is a one-stop-shop for gifts."

T: *0845 300 1707* W: *www.fortnumandmason.com*

GOOD FOR...
...fresh picnics for stylish alfresco dining.
...corporate gifts such as stationery, wine or gift boxes.
...luxury hampers to suit all occasions and sentiments.

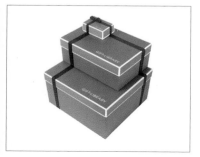

GIFT-LIBRARY.COM
A GIFTING COMPANY

"For the time-short shopper, Gift-Library.com is full of ideas with solutions to all your gifting needs."

T: *020 3080 0530* W: *www.gift-library.com*

GOOD FOR...
...taking the hassle out of gift-buying for time-short Londoners.
...finding luxury and unique gifts for all occasions.
...novelty gifts and homeware, diamonds and designer brands.

HAPPY BOX LONDON
A GIFTING COMPANY

"Quite simply – happiness in a box: it makes you happy; it makes them happy."

T: *020 7381 0803* W: *www.happyboxlondon.com*

GOOD FOR...

...choosing gifts online, and someone else beautifully
    wrapping and delivering it (no matter how last minute).
...creative corporate gifts that reflect brands and beliefs.

MOUNT STREET PRINTERS
A SPECIALIST STATIONER

"Established in 1981, Mount Street has been delivering exceptional stationery ever since."

T: *020 7409 0303* W: *www.mountstreetprinters.com*

GOOD FOR...

...a full range of printing methods.
...exquisite personalised wedding stationery.
...top quality off-the-shelf stationery.

MOYSES STEVENS
A FLORIST

"With 45 expert florists based around the globe, Moyses Stevens is a hub of innovation and design."

T: *020 8772 0094* W: *www.moysesflowers.co.uk*

GOOD FOR...

...guidance on choosing wedding flowers and themes.
...adding drama and style to large scale events.
...wedding displays, bouquets and button holes.

PAUL ANTONIO SCRIBE
A CALLIGRAPHER

"Paul Antonio is a perfectionist and will make sure you dot your 'i's and cross your 't's."

T: *020 7720 8883* W: *www.paulantonioscribe.com*

GOOD FOR...

...the most creative and beautiful calligraphy around.
...personalising invitations by hand for added wow factor.

PICCOLO PRESS

A SPECIALIST STATIONER

"Offering timeless skills, Piccolo Press can be relied upon for quality invitations and stationery."

T: *01667 454 508* W: *www.piccolopress.co.uk*

GOOD FOR...

...prestigious stationery requiring engraving or diestamping.

...top quality invitations with letterpress, thermography, blind embossing or foil blocking.

ROBBIE HONEY

A FLORIST

"Offering quality, creativity, and international credibility, Robbie Honey is a florist with finesse."

T: *020 7720 3777* W: *www.robbiehoney.com*

GOOD FOR...

...classic blooms for a traditional wedding.

...bringing a riot of colour to a spectacular event.

...creative arrangements to enhance themes and designs.

ROB VAN HELDEN

A FLORIST

"Rob Van Helden is renowned for inimitable displays and his resultant, impressive client list."

T: *020 7720 6774* W: *www.rvhfloraldesign.com*

GOOD FOR...

...sumptuous and stylish arrangements to amaze.

...classically simple displays through to flamboyant spectacles.

...a floral prop hire service.

SOPHIE HANNA

A FLORIST

"A visit to Covent Garden Flower Market with Sophie Hanna is an exquisite event in itself."

T: *020 7720 0841* W: *www.sophiehannaflowers.com*

GOOD FOR...

...a trip to the flower market to decide on colour schemes.

...spectacular and unique floral displays to reflect any themes.

...the church, the reception, the bride and the buttonholes.

U´LUVKA
A GIFTING COMPANY

"An exceptional premium vodka, an U´luvka set makes for a luxurious and memorable corporate gift."

T: *020 7602 7788* W: *www.uluvka.com*

GOOD FOR...
...a luxury corporate gift with a difference.
...engraving the bottles for personalisation and branding.
...a good value gift that's indulgent and memorable.

THE WALTON STREET STATIONERY COMPANY
A SPECIALIST STATIONER

"The Walton Street Stationery Company offer a range of top quality invitations."

T: *020 7589 0000* W: *www.waltonstreetstationery.com*

GOOD FOR...
...bespoke invitations and personal stationery for all occasions.
...personal guidance, advice and full design service in-store.

WREN PRESS
A SPECIALIST STATIONER

"An established British business, The Wren Press offers a comprehensive range of luxury stationery."

T: *020 7351 5887* W: *www.wrenpress.co.uk*

GOOD FOR...
...contemporary wedding invitations with edge.
...invitations and stationery of the finest quality.
...unique fonts and shades.

HAIR SALONS

HEALTH & FITNESS

SPAS

GET THE LOOK

Party planning can take its toll on one's appearance: before you've had your first sip of Champagne, you can already look hungover.

So whether for a particular occasion or just to keep yourself looking and feeling good as you battle through London life, here are the experts to call.

AGUA SPA
A SPA

"Agua offers complete escapism; a place to relax, unwind, forget and fortify."

---

50 Berners Street, London W1T 3NG
T: *020 7300 1414* W: *www.sandersonlondon.com*

GOOD FOR...
...a combination of ancient and modern techniques.
...an indulgent, and soothing urban sanctuary.

BEAUTYWORKSWEST
A SPA

"Blending beauty and science, BWW is a one-stop shop for all your health and beauty needs."

8/9 Lambton Place, London W11 2SH
T: *020 7221 2248* W: *www.beautyworkswest.com*

GOOD FOR...
...body buffing, nails and tans, facials, pampering and preening.
...state-of-the-art technology and cutting-edge treatments.

BROOKS & BROOKS
A HAIR SALON

"A boutique salon in Bloomsbury, Brooks & Brooks has won hairdresser of the year three times. "

13-15 Sicilian Avenue, London WC1A 2QH
T: *020 7405 8111* W: *www.brooksandbrooks.co.uk*

GOOD FOR...
...versatile styles that are easy to manage.
...visiting on a Sunday and late appointments during the week.

THE CHAPEL
A HAIR SALON

"The multi award-winning Chapel delivers a complete package of relaxation and service."

---

394 - 396 St John Street, London EC1V 4NJ
T: *020 7520 0460* W: *www.thechapel.co.uk*

GOOD FOR...
...bespoke hair appointments charged by time, not treatments.
...being treated as a guest, not just another customer.

COWSHED
A SPA

"Combining a unique home-grown, rustic ambiance with organic products."

Shoreditch House, Ebor Street, London E1 6AW
T: *020 7749 4531* W: *www.cowshedonline.com*

GOOD FOR...
...treatments and Champagne with a group of girlfriends.
...stylishly packed corporate gifts.

DANIEL GALVIN
A HAIR SALON

"Daniel Galvin is a celebrity salon offering advanced treatments and styling in a chic and spacious setting."

58-60 George Street, London W1U 7ET
T: *020 7486 9661* W: *www.danielgalvin.com*

GOOD FOR...
...beauty services from manicures to eyelash extensions.
...specialist colour services, renowned the world over.

DANIEL HERSHESON
A HAIR SALON

"Operates at the cutting edge in every respect, and even fits into your shopping schedule."

Harvey Nichols, 109 - 125 Knightsbridge, London SW1X 7RJ
T: *020 7201 8797* W: *www.danielhersheson.com*

GOOD FOR...
...a permanent blow-dry to manage frizz.
...fashion-forward hair and trend-setting treatments.

GENTLEMEN'S TONIC
A SPA

"A stylish barbershop offering comprehensive, exceptional grooming services."

31A Bruton Place, London W1J 6NN
T: *020 7432 6441* W: *www.gentlemenstonic.com*

GOOD FOR...
...LCD screens in each private hair-cutting station.
...all the products and accessories a modern man needs.

HARI'S
A HAIR SALON

"A sleek salon seeing to the tresses of South Kensington's glossiest."

305 Brompton Road, London, SW3 2DY
T: *020 7581 5211* W: *www.harissalon.com*

GOOD FOR...
...Brazilian blow-dries, extensions and straightening.
...customised, fashion-inspired manicures and pedicures.

JOHN FRIEDA
A HAIR SALON

"Offering discreet oases of calm, for celebrities and discerning consumers who demand the best."

4 Aldford Street, London W1
T: *020 7491 0840* W: *www.johnfrieda.co.uk*

GOOD FOR...
...consistent excellence with world-renowned experts.
...pre-party hair and nails to look and feel your very best.

KELL SKÖTT HAIRCARE
A HAIR SALON

"Unpretentious and affordable, Kell Skött Haircare is a refreshing addition to West London's salon scene."

2-4 Lambton Place, London W11 2SH
T: *020 7229 1671* W: *www.kellskotthaircare.com*

GOOD FOR...
...a walk-in blow-dry service.
...hair styling, colour and homemade brownies to die for.

LOMAX BESPOKE HEALTH
A PERSONAL TRAINER, GYM & NUTRITIONIST

"A health concierge company that will bullet-proof body and mind against London life."

Lomax Victoria, 59 Buckingham Gate, London SW1E 6AJ
T: *08715 120 770* W: *www.lomaxpt.com*

GOOD FOR...
...in home trainers and a pay-as-you-go gym and health hub.
...nutritional advice, meal planning and food delivery.

SERVICES

MANDARIN ORIENTAL
A SPA

"Professional and renowned, this spa offers a hidden haven in which to relax and unwind."

Mandarin Oriental, 66 Knightsbridge, London SW1X 7LA
T: *020 7235 2000* W: *www.mandarinoriental.com/london/spa*

GOOD FOR...
...indigenous practices to combat modern stresses.
...a vitality pool, steam room and Zen colour therapy room.

PAUL EDMONDS
A HAIR SALON

"If you're shopping in Knightsbridge, this salon is a perfect retreat to get a (root) lift."

217 Brompton Road, London SW3 2EJ
T: *020 7589 5958* W: *www.pauledmonds.com*

GOOD FOR...
...cuts and colours to suit you and your lifestyle.
...a private room for ultimate luxury and privacy.

PHILIP KINGSLEY
A HAIR CLINIC

"Philip Kingsley is a 'hair doctor' keeping hair healthy from root to tip, in the clinic or at home."

54 Green Street, London W1K 6RU
T: *020 7629 4004* W: *www.philipkingsley.co.uk*

GOOD FOR...
...a clinic with a unique approach to all hair and scalp
   conditions by a world renowned, highly qualified team.

TAYLOR TAYLOR LONDON
A HAIR SALON

"Taking your beauty into their hands, Taylor Taylor is regularly voted one of Europe's leading salons."

137 Commercial Street, London E1 6BJ
T: *020 7377 2737* W: *www.taylortaylorlondon.com*

GOOD FOR...
...creative styling to ensure glamorous hair with impact.
...express-highlights to look twice as good in half the time.

VENUE INFORMATION CHART
& INDEX

VENUE INFO

VENUE NAME	FUNCTION ROOMS*	MAXIMUM CAPACITY**	PRIVATE DINING***	CUISINE	NEAREST TUBE	CIVIL CEREMONIES	OUTSIDE SPACE	PAGE
30 Pavilion Road	3	120 / 240	26, 120	British	Knightsbridge	Y	N	26
40 | 30 at The Gherkin	5	90 / 260	12, 15	French	Aldgate	Y	N	27
Adam Street	5	80 / 350	12, 60, 80	British	Charing Cross	Y	N	27
All Star Lanes	2	- / 350	N/A	American	Bayswater	N	N	28
Almada	2	155 / 200	155	Mod. European	Green Park	N	N	28
Altitude London	7	400 / 1,200	80, 95, 240, 400	British	Pimlico	Y	N	29
Amika	4	- / 600	N/A	N/A	High St Ken.	N	N	29
aqua kyoto	3	110 / 200	10, 110	Japanese	Oxford Circus	Y	Y	30
Arch London, The	3	40 / 50	10, 18, 30	Mod. European	Marble Arch	N	N	30
Attic, The	1	- / 80	N/A	Canapés	South Quays DLR	N	N	31
Automat	N/A	N/A	N/A	American	Green Park	N	N	31
Baltic	2	150 / 400	33, 150	East. European	Southwark	N	N	32
Barrafina	N/A	N/A	N/A	Tapas	Tottenham Ct Rd	N	Y	32
Barts	1	50 / 80	50	N/A	Sloane Square	Y	Y	33
Bathhouse, The	2	120 / 220	120	Mod. European	Liverpool Street	N	N	33
Battery Club	2	200 / 220	N/A	Mod. European	Canary Wharf	Y	N	34
Beaufort House	3	150 / 150	22, 100, 150	Mod. European	Sloane Square	Y	Y	34
Bentley's Oyster Bar & Grill	2	60 / 100	14, 60	Seafood	Piccadilly Circus	N	Y	35
Berkeley, The	6	200 / 400	10, 14, 18, 20, 200	French, Tea	Hyde Park Corner	Y	Y	35
Big Easy, The	1	162 / -	N/A	American	South Kensington	N	Y	36
Bisley Shooting Ground	3	- / 300	N/A	British	Brookwood	N	Y	36
Blues Kitchen, The	1	150 / 300	N/A	American	Camden Town	N	N	37
Bocca di Lupo	2	60 / -	32, 60	Italian	Piccadilly Circus	N	N	37
Boisdale	2	140 / 230	22, 140	British	Victoria	Y	Y	38
Boundary	2	136 / 160	35, 136	French	Old Street	N	Y	38
Brewery, The	6	750 / 1,000	N/A	Flex. catering	Moorgate	Y	N	39
Brompton Club, The	4	100 / 350	20, 50, 100	Mod. European	South Kensington	N	N	39
Brown's Hotel	6	72 / 120	6, 8, 12, 40, 72	British	Green Park	Y	N	40
Buen Ayre	N/A	34 / -	N/A	Steak	Bethnal Green	N	N	40
Café de Paris	4	260 / 715	260	Mod. European	Piccadilly Circus	Y	N	41
Café Luc	1	100 / 150	100	French	Baker Street	N	N	41
Caravan	2	60 / 120	12, 60	Mod. European	Farringdon	N	Y	42
Cecconi's	1	20 / -	20	Italian	Green Park	N	N	42
China White	4	50 / 575	50	Pan Asian	Oxford Circus	N	N	43
Cinnamon Club, The	5	220 / 500	30, 60, 130, 220	Indian	St James's Park	Y	N	43
Circus	1	140 / 300	N/A	Pan Asian	Covent Garden	N	N	44
City Golf	1	- / 250	N/A	Flex. catering	Bank	N	N	44
Claridge's	10	240 / 450	6,20,50,96,120,240	British, Tea	Bond Street	Y	N	45
Connaught, The	7	120 / 200	12, 20, 60, 120	French, Tea	Bond Street	Y	N	45

VENUE NAME	FUNCTION ROOMS*	MAXIMUM CAPACITY**	PRIVATE DINING***	CUISINE	NEAREST TUBE	CIVIL CEREMONIES	OUTSIDE SPACE	PAGE
Corrigan's	4	70 / -	6, 12, 30, 70	British	Marble Arch	N	N	46
Crazy Bear	4	40 / 135	40	Pan Asian	Covent Garden	N	N	46
Cuckoo Club, The	2	80 / 300	80	Mod. European	Piccadilly Circus	N	N	47
Daphne's	1	40 / 50	40	Italian	South Kensington	N	Y	47
Dean St Townhouse	1	12 / 20	12	Mod. European	Leicester Square	N	Y	48
Deck, The	1	80 / 120	80	Flex. catering	Waterloo	Y	Y	48
Dinner	1	10 / -	10	British	Knightsbridge	N	N	49
Dishoom	1	80 / 80	80	Indian	Leicester Square	N	Y	49
Dorchester, The	11	500 / 1,000	12, 34, 60, 140, 500	French, Cantonese	Hyde Park Corner	Y	N	50
Dukes Hotel	4	60 / 120	12, 14, 60	British	Green Park	Y	Y	50
E&O	1	18 / -	18	Pan Asian	Ladbroke Grove	N	Y	51
EDF Energy London Eye	32	- / 25	N/A	Flex. catering	Waterloo	Y	N	51
Embassy London	4	- / 450	N/A	Mod. European	Green Park	N	Y	52
Franco's	3	70 / 120	18, 30, 70	Italian	Green Park	N	Y	52
Galvin at Windows	2	120 / 150	30, 120	French	Hyde Park Corner	Y	N	53
Gray's Inn	6	188 / 350	12, 16, 70, 80, 188	Flex. catering	Chancery Lane	Y	Y	53
Grazing Goat, The	2	60 / 100	32, 60	British	Marble Arch	N	Y	54
Hakkasan Mayfair	2	220 / 275	14, 220	Chinese	Green Park	N	N	54
Hawksmoor	1	14 / -	14	Steak	Sh'ditch High St	N	N	55
Hibiscus	2	45 / -	18, 45	French	Oxford Circus	N	N	55
HIX Soho	3	80 / 220	10, 36, 80	British	Piccadilly Circus	N	N	56
Home House	5	80 / 200	22, 80	Mod. European	Marble Arch	Y	Y	56
Hospital Club, The	10	150 / 300	8,12,18,30,35,150	British	Covent Garden	Y	Y	57
Hurlingham Club, The	7	1,000 / 1,200	14,60,95,350,1,000	British	Putney Bridge	Y	Y	57
IndigO2	3	1,623 / -	N/A	Flex. catering	North Greenwich	N	N	58
Inner Temple	5	200 / 400	12, 30, 50, 90, 200	Flex. catering	Temple	Y	Y	58
Ivy, The	1	60 / 120	60	British	Leicester Square	N	N	59
J Sheekey	0	6 / -	N/A	British, Seafood	Leicester Square	N	N	59
King Pin Suite, The	2	- / 250	N/A	American	Russell Square	N	N	60
Kopapa	1	60 / 80	60	Mod. European	Covent Garden	N	N	60
Kosmopol	2	- / 120	N/A	Bar snacks	Gloucester Road	N	N	61
Landmark, The	11	504 / 750	N/A	British, Tea	Marylebone	Y	Y	61
Le Caprice	0	8 / -	N/A	Mod. European	Green Park	N	N	62
Ledbury, The	N/A	N/A	N/A	British	Westbourne Park	N	Y	62
Les Deux Salons	3	150 / 300	10, 25, 150	French	Charing Cross	N	N	63
Lucky Voice	10	- / 130	N/A	Pizza, Bar snacks	Oxford Circus	N	N	63
Lutyens	4	120 / 250	6, 12, 16, 26, 120	French, Seafood	Blackfriars	N	N	64
Madame Tussauds	5	380 / 1,000	380	Flex. catering	Baker Street	N	N	64
Maddox	4	80 / 352	20, 80	Mod. European	Oxford Circus	N	Y	65

VENUE NAME	FUNCTION ROOMS*	MAXIMUM CAPACITY**	PRIVATE DINING***	CUISINE	NEAREST TUBE	CIVIL CEREMONIES	OUTSIDE SPACE	PAGE
Madison	2	120 / 250	120	British	St Paul's	Y	Y	65
Maggie's	1	- / 180	N/A	N/A	South Kensington	N	N	66
Mahiki	2	- / 350	N/A	Pan Asian	Green Park	N	N	66
J Sheekey	7	250 / 400	30, 60, 120, 250	British, French	Knightsbridge	Y	Y	67
Mews of Mayfair	5	150 / 350	16, 28, 70, 150	Mod. European	Bond Street	N	Y	67
Middle Temple Hall	4	500 / -	N/A	Flex. catering	Temple	Y	Y	68
Min Jiang	1	80 / -	20, 80	Chinese	High St Ken.	N	N	68
Mint Leaf Lounge & Restaurant	3	90 / 300	60, 90	Indian	Bank	Y	N	69
Mint Leaf Restaurant & Bar	2	240 / 450	65, 240	Indian	Piccadilly Circus	Y	N	69
Morton's	4	48 / 70	24, 48	French, Italian	Bond Street	N	Y	70
Movida	3	- / 400	N/A	N/A	Oxford Circus	N	N	70
Nobu London	2	200 / 400	50, 200	Japanese	Hyde Park Corner	N	N	71
Number Sixteen	1	10 / 50	10	British, Tea	South Kensington	Y	Y	71
Old Billingsgate	3	1,200 / 2,400	N/A	Flex. catering	Monument	N	Y	72
Old Queen's Head, The	2	100 / 170	60, 100	Pub fare	Angel	N	N	72
One Aldwych	6	80 / 180	80	British	Covent Garden	Y	N	73
Opera Tavern	1	40 / -	40	Tapas	Covent Garden	N	N	73
Orange, The	5	70 / 120	12, 18, 25, 40, 70	British, European	Sloane Square	N	N	74
OXO Tower	3	320 / 700	65, 150, 320	Mod. European	Waterloo	Y	Y	74
Palm, The	2	120 / 150	50, 120	American, Steak	Knightsbridge	N	N	75
Pantechnicon	3	46 / 80	14, 20, 46	British	Knightsbridge	N	N	75
Paradise by Way of Kensal Green	5	70 / 500	16, 20, 70	British	Kensal Green / Kensal Rise	Y	Y	76
Pizza East	1	18 / -	18	Pizza, Italian	Sh'ditch High St	N	N	76
Polpo	N/A	N/A	N/A	Italian	Piccadilly Circus	N	N	77
Portrait Restaurant	1	80 / 200	N/A	British, Tea	Charing Cross	N	N	77
Proud Cabaret	1	240 / 330	240	British	Monument	N	N	78
Proud2	5	300 / 3,500	N/A	N/A	North Greenwich	Y	N	78
Providores & Tapa Room, The	1	40 / -	40	Fusion	Bond Street	N	N	79
Public	2	- / 450	N/A	N/A	Fulham Broadway	N	N	79
Quintessentially Soho at the House of St Barnabas	8	50 / 300	N/A	Flex. catering	Tottenham Ct Rd	N	Y	80
Quo Vadis	3	36 / 80	12, 24, 36	British	Tottenham Ct Rd	N	Y	80
Raffles	2	- / 220	N/A	N/A	South Kensington	N	N	81
Redhook	1	64 / 150	14, 64	Steak, Seafood	Farringdon	N	N	81
Ritz, The	6	60 / 120	16, 24, 30, 60	British	Green Park	Y	Y	82

VENUE NAME	FUNCTION ROOMS*	MAXIMUM CAPACITY**	PRIVATE DINING***	CUISINE	NEAREST TUBE	OUTSIDE SPACE	CIVIL CEREMONIES	PAGE
River Café	1	18 / -	18	Italian	Hammersmith	N	Y	82
Roast	1	120 / 220	120	British	London Bridge	Y	N	83
Roka	1	88 / -	88	Japanese	Goodge Street	N	Y	83
Roof Gardens & Babylon, The	3	180 / 500	12, 28, 180	British	High St Ken.	Y	Y	84
Salt Yard	1	40 / -	40	Tapas	Goodge Street	N	N	84
Sanctum Soho Hotel	3	70 / 120	70	British, Tea	Piccadilly Circus	N	Y	85
Sanderson	4	40 / 80	22, 40	Malaysian, Tea	Goodge Street	N	Y	85
Savoy, The	6	50 / 80	10,12,18,24,30,50	British, French	Charing Cross	Y	N	86
Scott's	1	40 / 50	40	British, Seafood	Bond Street	N	Y	86
Serpentine Gallery	1	70 / 150	N/A	Flex. catering	South Kensington	N	Y	87
Shoreditch House	3	180 / 200	90, 180	British	Sh'ditch High St	Y	Y	87
Shoreditch Town Hall	6	400 / 800	N/A	Flex. catering	Old Street	Y	N	88
Simpson's-in-the-Strand	2	120 / 250	50, 120	British	Charing Cross	Y	N	88
sketch	5	150 / 650	24, 50, 50, 150	Fusion	Oxford Circus	Y	N	89
SkyLounge	1	60 / 240	60	British	Tower Hill	Y	Y	89
Soho Hotel, The	6	70 / 300	10, 20, 50, 70	British, Tea	Tottenham Ct Rd	Y	N	90
Soho House	4	60 / 80	42	British	Tottenham Ct Rd	Y	Y	90
Somerset House	11	550 / 1,500	50, 80, 100, 250, 550	Flex. catering	Charing Cross	Y	Y	91
Square, The	2	80 / -	18, 80	Mod. European	Green Park	N	N	91
St John Bar & Restaurant	2	110 / 130	18, 110	Nose-to-Tail	Barbican	N	N	92
St Martins Lane	3	96 / 180	48, 96	Asian-Latino	Leicester Square	Y	Y	92
Stafford London by Kempinski	5	44 / 75	8, 12, 38, 44	British	Green Park	N	Y	93
Summerhouse, The	1	50 / 70	50	British	Warwick Avenue	N	Y	93
Sumosan	2	120 / 200	32, 120	Japanese	Green Park	N	N	94
supperclub	1	155 / 500	155	Mod. European	Ladbroke Grove	N	Y	94
Tamarind	1	84 / -	84	Indian	Green Park	N	Y	95
Thomas Cubitt, The	4	42 / 120	12, 20, 30, 42	British	Victoria	N	N	95
Tom's Kitchen	2	40 / 75	22, 40	British	South Kensington	N	N	96
Tramp	2	80 / 200	80	Mod. European	Piccadilly Circus	N	N	96
V&A, The	3	400 / 600	230, 400	Flex. catering	South Kensington	N	Y	97
Vista	5	420 / 520	18, 24, 48, 150, 180	Mod. European	Charing Cross	Y	Y	97
Whisky Mist	2	- / 240	N/A	N/A	Hyde Park Corner	N	N	98
Wolseley, The	1	12 / -	12	European	Green Park	N	N	98
Zafferano	1	20 / -	20	Italian	Knightsbridge	N	N	99
Zuma	2	14 / -	12, 14	Japanese	Knightsbridge	N	Y	99

*** Number of rooms available for private hire; ** Seated / Standing;
*** Capacities for sit down private dining**

INDEX